# Target Europe

*Interpreting the times and
seasons of God's kingdom
in the lands and
islands of Europe and
the challenge for today*

## Roger and Sue Mitchell

**Sovereign World**

Sovereign World Ltd
PO Box 777
Tonbridge
Kent TN11 0ZS
England

Unless otherwise stated, all Scripture quotations are taken from the New
American Standard Version © The Lockman Foundation 1960, 1963,
1968, 1971, 1973, 1975, 1977. All rights reserved.

Quotations are also taken from the New King James Version (NKJV),
copyright © 1983 by Thomas Nelson, Inc.

ISBN 1 85240 303 9

The publishers aim to produce books which will help to extend and
build up the Kingdom of God. We do not necessarily agree with every
view expressed by the author, or with every interpretation of Scripture
expressed. We expect each reader to make his/her judgement in the
light of their own understanding of God's Word and in an attitude of
Christian love and fellowship.

Typeset by CRB Associates, Reepham, Norfolk.
Printed in England by Clays Ltd, St Ives plc.

# What Others Are Saying About *Target Europe*

'In this book you can hear the intensity of the "heart-of-Elijah" father-leadership that God is restoring back to the Church in this time and for this hour in Europe. Only someone whose heart is truly turned to the children can write words in a book like this – words which have been waiting to be released through a vessel which not only *carries* a message of fatherhood, but whose life and ministry have literally *incarnated* the message and spirit of Elijah. Get ready for impartation, not only for information and revelation.'                    ***George P. Bakalov***

Founder/Senior Pastor, Breakthrough Christian Center, Bulgaria

'Empowering and inspiring – Roger and Sue Mitchell are passionately concerned about the challenge of the coming harvest and their latest book brings much-needed insight for every 21st Century disciple.'

***David Bishop***
Chairman, Building Together, UK

'Is Europe still a mission field? Yes it is. Wherever thousands of towns and villages without a single church exist, there is a mission field. It means that the church of Jesus around the world needs to be praying for it. Through years of knowing and working with Roger and Sue Mitchell I can confirm that whatever is needed for the completion of the Great Commission, they will do. Their heart and passion for the kingdom is a blessing for those around them. I believe this book will bless you, your church with passion, vision and understanding of the mission field and mission needs.'

***Amaury Braga Junior***
Dawn Prayer Co-ordinator for Latin America, Brazil

'This is a brilliantly written, passionate, whirlwind tour through the European story that provides a convincing explanation for the spiritual development of the European world as we know it and the lessons for our future. Ambitious and courageous, this is an attempt to uncover nothing less than the redemptive purpose of a continent. After reading the first chapter, you won't be able to put it down.'                    ***John Dawson***

Founder, International Reconciliation Coalition, New Zealand and USA

'Roger and Sue Mitchell are called of God to see that Europe comes to the destiny He created it for. They have done a great service to the body of Christ by giving us the strategic information we as intercessors need to pray and see this great continent experience another reformation.'

***Cindy Jacobs***
Founder/President, Generals of Intercession, USA

'Travelling through Europe one finds a lot of people who are hungry for God and would like to go deeper in their experience with Him. However, many find that they cannot "press through" or "pray through". Usually in such circumstances the answer lies in what has happened in their past history. What Roger and Sue Mitchell have done is to dig back into the history of the land to find the roots of the problems, as well as the old forgotten ways. This book is definitely a key to unlocking doors that have remained shut until today. I believe that as people digest these truths there will be a liberty to cross bridges hitherto uncrossed. May the Lord bless this work.'                                              *Pastor John Mulinde*

World Trumpet Mission, Kampala, Uganda

'This book is a must read for anyone with a heart for Europe. It implants in the minds of those reading a strategy of prayer to break the power of captivity in this region of the earth and release resurrection power and restoration. This book has key understanding for the release of Harvest throughout Europe. God's purpose in Europe has never come into prophetic fulfillment. This is a roadmap on how to get there.'     *Dr Chuck D. Pierce*

President, Glory of Zion International, USA

'In *Target Europe*, Roger and Sue have articulated and summarised thoughts and actions that the Holy Spirit has been opening up in His praying, prophetic people over the last decade. It provides a much-needed theological base for issues such as "the land" and "praying into nations' wounded history". It is a book for praying practitioners, spiritual interventionists and those who love Europe and want to see the way cleared for revival across the continent. It's also a real good read!'     *John Pressdee*

Leader of Prayer Expeditions, UK

'Humble of heart and strong in the Lord are the main characteristics of these two precious people I have had the privilege to come into relationship with. I cannot speak of Roger without hearing these words in my spirit: Apostle of reconciliation! I believe his is a very important ministry for the sake of Europe. Sue, a prophetess and a fiery lioness, is none other than a spiritual mother for this continent. I am convinced their book will be a great challenge to its readers. It will undoubtedly stir up compassion within your heart and revive your passion for Christ.'     *Samuel Rhein*

Leadership team of Rhein–Rhone network, France

'Roger and Sue's ministry is in many ways that of the forerunner. In their new book they are giving vital keys for a spiritual breakthrough in Europe. Let's get a new stirring of God in our hearts and use the deep insight and revelation that is offered to us here. Some of the issues raised might not be common sense today, but surely will be tomorrow.'

*Michael Schiffmann*
Target Europe and Director of the Christian Training Center
Hanover, Germany

'Perceptive, prophetic, at times hard-hitting, but throughout faith-inspiring. *Target Europe* is an essential read for all who are asking "where to from here?", and for those who have already heard the Holy Spirit say "Europe" this book will bring a level of understanding that will both channel and fuel growing convictions.' *Martin Scott*
Sowing Seeds For Revival, UK

'Roger and Sue Mitchell are a gift from God to the entire Church. Their passion for God is used by Him to touch multitudes all over the world. Their passion for reconciliation has built bridges where there used to be none and where today grace crosses freely and generously. Their book *Target Europe* is a glimpse into their hearts which reflects the heart of God for Europe. Read, be encouraged and go and change the world.'

*Ed Silvoso*
Author of *Prayer Evangelism*
President, Harvest Evangelism, Inc., Argentina and USA

'What Roger and Sue Mitchell are seeing and doing has, for many years now, been at the forefront of God's unfolding purposes on the earth. They have paid a price to continually press into new and uncharted territory. They have been a blessing to so many people who have been able to enter into the new places in God they have pioneered. *Target Europe* is a distillation of the wisdom, the sight and the cost they have gathered over many years. As such it is a great gift to the body of Christ, an essential word for this time for all who carry in their heart the nations of Europe.'

*James Thwaites*
Author of *Church Beyond the Congregation*, Australia

'Is the day for God's glory to once again envelope Europe now dawning? Roger and Sue Mitchell are convinced that it is, and their thorough, mature, and prophetic analysis of the reasons for this should dispel all possible doubts and raise our faith to a new level! *Target Europe* is truly a vital message for our times.' *Dr C. Peter Wagner*
Chancellor, Wagner Leadership Institute, USA

*With great gratitude
to those with whom we shared life and
biblical exploration for over 20 years
in the Ichthus team.*

# Contents

# Preface

A generation is rising with their hearts turned to the fathers. Their discipleship has been erratic and many of them are right now struggling to overcome the evil one. Most of them do not have the language to express much of what is within them, but it is my conviction that we are yet to see some of the greatest treasures contained in earthen vessels. These young men and women are intercessory signs of what it means to stand in the gap with God. In their fight with the flesh and the devil they have persevered, working with the grace that God has given them; they are becoming righteous women and men and their prayers will be powerful and effective. They are a generation of resurrection; in their struggle with sin they are learning to die to themselves and to wait upon the Father to vindicate them in resurrection. To use authorial language, this rising generation has been born to participate in this *fourth day*! Could it be that many who are standing today will not taste death until they see the Son of Man coming in His Kingdom? I believe so! The Lord is waiting for His enemies to be made a footstool for His feet. It is the destiny of the Church to 'furniture' God's enemies. God will do it but He will do it in partnership with those who volunteer freely in the day of power – the fourth day! I commend this book to you, not because it is written by my friends, or because Roger and Sue have got it all sorted – they have not! Rather I commend this book because I believe in it we can hear what the Spirit is saying to the Church. Its insights have been forged on the anvil of prophetic biblical reflection. For too long the prophetic has been a smouldering wick snuffed out. The day has changed; apostolic and prophetic partnership will again be the foundation of a re-formed Church. The old and the new are on a collision course with one another. The Kingdom is coming! This book is the work of disciples of the Kingdom of heaven who are bringing out of their treasure things old and new. This is not a book of answers, but a collection of wisdom, insights and prophetic revelations shared. It is a book that helps us to locate ourselves in the history of God; to consider our destiny and purpose in relation to the creation and redemption instructions. Church, let's see our continent routed by the gospel of the Kingdom.

**Come on!**

*Anonymous, July 2001*
On behalf of the nameless and
faceless rising generation.

# Chapter 1

## It's the Third Day!

Christian prophets from many sources have been declaring it to be the third day. For some this is simply a response to the third millennium since Christ, and the recognition that *'with the Lord a thousand years is but one day'*. But for others there is a more profoundly historical recognition that we have entered a new day in the progress of the Kingdom of God into all the earth. From this perspective the first day was the Jewish mission and lasted for barely 100 years. But what a century that was! Served by the leadership of the Jewish apostles and their disciples the gospel was taken throughout the then known world, most strategically into Europe where it took root to great effect and profoundly transformed the history of the ensuing 2000 years. If only the Gentile mission had remained as pure and been so rapidly productive, the history of the progress of the Kingdom of God on planet Earth would have been very different. However, the second day of world mission was another story. Almost exclusively European, it was some 1500 years before it issued in any real missionary vision for the rest of the world. In Europe the gospel became so mixed with the motives of empire and the political aspirations of the rich and powerful that even then it was another 400 years before the seed of the gospel took root abroad to the degree that it resulted in massive growth in what we could call biblical Holy Spirit Christianity. So the second day of world mission lasted for close to 2000 years. But despite the mixture the seed has proved to be good. So good that the multiplication of the living Church outside of Europe, in those regions and continents alluded to by Jesus as *'the uttermost parts of the earth'* has reached unprecedented proportions. The Church in South America, Africa, and Asia is much larger than the now shrinking Church in Europe.

From this perspective the third day of world mission has been dawning upon us in the last half century and is only now ready to have its full impact on the European world. To some extent this is so because of the part played by the ex-colonial, mainly European nations in the farthest parts of the earth from Jerusalem like the USA, Canada, Australia and New Zealand. They have had a strategic mid-way role in the dawning of this third day, since they are geographically part of it but are (nevertheless) culturally and historically linked to the second day of world mission. What they do share with the rising initiative of the leadership of the third day Church is a vision to re-evangelise Europe. Along with the leaders of the Church in South America, Africa and Asia they find themselves responding to the great commission of Jesus *'to go into all the world and preach the gospel'* by looking back to the Middle East, and 'Jerusalem, Judea and Samaria' where it all began. But in between is the one continent where the gospel of the Kingdom of God is not expanding, yet it is the continent from where the good seed came to them. This continent, Europe, with its forty-eight or so nations, has become the primary target of world mission for the third day Church.

## Words and Signs from the Third Day Church

In the late 1980s several thriving churches in the town of Uberlandia, Brazil, who had been working together in unity out of the desire to reach their city, were interrupted by a prophecy from one of their leaders. Revival was coming to Europe and they were to go and help. Then the Brazilian Church would go together with the converts into the so-called 10/40 Window. Recognising a word from God they lost no time in setting apart their best leaders and sending them to the UK: men like Paulo Borges, 'Arry Skates and Marcos Barros. They came in the early 1990s first of all to London where we remember meeting them at a local leadership conference. We could just about understand their desire for partnership in mission to the 10/40 Window, but at first could make no sense of their talk of coming to help us with revival in the UK. To be honest, the idea of missionaries from South America coming **to** us was outside our paradigm of thought. Several years later on a mission in Glasgow we met them again. By this time the Church in Britain had been touched by the DAWN vision to Disciple A Whole Nation (itself birthed in the Philippines) as well as by a new and highly significant move of the Spirit. A bunch of us leaders from towns and regions throughout the UK had realised that something new was about to happen and had begun to meet up regularly to encourage one another and compare notes (this has now become what is known as Building Together). In common with many others we had between us found our way to revival situations like those in Korea and Argentina and had been to Toronto to discover their experience of the move of God we were enjoying here. Now the significance of the Brazilians coming was more obvious. God was about to give Europe a new opportunity for the gospel, and the initiative was coming from outside Europe. Having given up on London for the time being our Brazilian friends had moved to Edinburgh where they were gathering leaders from across the city to pray. Since then numerous other third day church initiatives have taken place. Brazilian missionaries are helping the Church all over the UK and increasingly in the rest of Europe. Initiatives from Argentina, Columbia and Costa Rica are well known. The catalogue of third day church initiatives into Europe is already too numerous to list. Men like Willy Soanes from India, 'The Heavenly Man' from China (see also p. 175) and of course Paul Yonggi Cho from Korea are becoming Christian household names.

Probably the one that sums them all up the most is the initiative of John Mulinde of Uganda. His story is by now well known. In the mid nineties God spoke to him, calling him to make a covenant for his nation and then to call other leaders to join him, that whether they lived or died, Uganda would be saved. Obedient to the heavenly vision they saw rapid changes for good in their nation. But then the Lord spoke a second time. In a dream John saw a map of Europe covered in darkness. Then flames of revival began to break through, but then again the darkness overcame them. But as John prayed he saw the flames re-emerge and push the darkness right back. His response was to call together his Ugandan colleagues to make a covenant. This time for Europe, that whether they lived or died Europe would be saved. Since then they have been coming to many parts of Europe at great personal cost to work together with European leaders to encourage them to give themselves with renewed faith and to make the same covenant.

## World Prayer Movement

The last ten years has seen an explosion of prayer on the earth. Heaven only knows the exact process that led to such an outbreak, but countless unsung spiritual heroes and heroines who have been the Annas and Simeons of our time certainly lie behind it. But probably all will agree that the Korean Church has had a large part to play with its many prayer mountains and all night prayer vigils. In 1993, intercession leaders from all over the world met on one such prayer mountain outside Seoul, Korea. They were representatives of the then-called Spiritual Warfare Network, led by Dr C. Peter Wagner, the co-ordinator of the Prayer Track of the AD2000 movement. Out from this set of relationships came several strategic initiatives which helped both to ignite and measure this explosion. Within just a few years Dr Wagner rightly described the world prayer movement as out of control. One of these contributing initiatives was the now famous 10/40 Window prayer initiative. While the spiritual battle in the least-reached regions of the world covered by the 10/40 Window is by no means over, and has in many ways just begun, the spiritual climate change accomplished there in the last ten years is extraordinary. Dr Wagner describes it in some detail in his chapter 'Prayer is shaking the world' in the book *The Queen's Domain* (Wagner Publications, 2000). He traces the almost bloodless dramatic end to apartheid, the massive increase in church planting among unreached people groups, the demise of Communism and the progress of the gospel in the face of Buddhism, Hinduism and Islam as part of the measure of success that the 'out of control' prayer movement has achieved.

As the decade progressed the sheer magnitude of the estimated numbers of intercessors harnessed to 'pray through the window' rose from 12 million in 1995 to 30 million in 1997, and up to 50 million in 1999. As the AD2000 movement came to an end with the advent of the twenty-first century, some of the key prophetic and apostolic leaders behind the 10/40 Window initiative began to hear the voice of God again, this time urging them to open a second window and to draw the focus of the world intercession movement into that. Not surprisingly, given the burden of the third day Church that we have already described, this is the 40/70 Window, and a new strategic prayer initiative is already underway to focus the prayers of the world Church onto Europe that is right in the centre of that window, together with the nations of the old Silk Road on through Central Asia and into China and the North of Korea and Japan. This initiative is also known as Target Europe and Target Silk Road. As far as Europe is concerned the prayers of possibly 50 million intercessors targeting our continent represents an extraordinary new opportunity for the gospel. True revival and a new destiny in the purposes of the King-dom of God on earth await us if we can embrace the moment.

## Questions That Must Be Asked

However, there are major questions facing us at such a time as this. The second day of world mission, the European day, took an unbelievable two millennia. Clearly the seed was good to survive that long and yield such fruit in the end. But not only did the gospel take a desperately long time to break forth from Europe, the continent is now in terrible disarray. The Church is shrinking and the culture has become starkly post-Christian – even increasingly like Sodom and Gomorrah. If the gospel has arrived with such vibrancy in the ends of the earth, yet the lands that held it for so long are in such disorder, what went wrong? On a visit to Korea a group of young Korean church leaders asked our advice. Several of them had been to the UK and seen the many huge church buildings which are now empty. They took me to see the brand new cinema organ being installed for worship in Seoul's equivalent to London's Westminster Central Hall. They asked me with tears, 'How can we avoid the same situation that you have in London today happening to us here in South Korea in a hundred years' time?' Surely this poignant question should cause us to consider carefully at this moment of new opportunity what we need to understand and, where possible, repent as Europeans for what has been done with the gospel on our continent to blunt its edge, slow down its progress and corrupt its content. We can be grateful for those of our fathers who remained true to it and lived and died for its progress and survival. But we cannot avoid our corporate responsibility. It may be that by the grace of God we can humbly identify those traits and seeds still present in the culture that we released with the good seed into the ends of the earth which will similarly impede its progress in our day. If we have courage enough this could prove to be in part the redemptive purpose of the history of the European continent. Even more it could mean that the renewed progress of the gospel in Europe that is surely coming will not fall prey to the same wiles of the devil second time round.

In short, we need an historical perspective and an end-time vision big enough to be able to hear and obey the voice of the Holy Spirit coming to the European continent – yes, the continent, not just the Church in Europe – and we need the grace to receive and learn from our spiritual children around the world as they turn their hearts back to their European fathers – their vocabulary, not just ours. This is the burden and intent of this book.

# Chapter 2

# The Second Day

The second day of world mission, or episode one of the Gentile mission, was, as we have said Europe's day. It is impossible in one chapter of a book like this to give an adequate, let alone complete, historical overview. What we will be attempting here is a revelational impression of the way in which the gospel progressed and was impeded as the Holy Spirit and His people partnered to get the good news of the Kingdom of God to the ends of the earth.

## The Gospel Arrives in Europe

The arrival of the Jewish mission into Europe was with great energy and power, characteristics which continued to mark the growing and developing Jew/Gentile apostolic partnership. The apostle Paul wrote of the mission into Thessalonica, Greece, that,

> '... our gospel did not come to you in word only, but also in power and in the Holy Spirit and with full conviction; just as you know what kind of men we proved to be among you for your sake. You also became imitators of us and of the Lord, having received the word in much tribulation with the joy of the Holy Spirit, so that you became an example to all the believers in Macedonia and Achaia. For the word of the Lord has sounded forth from you, not only in Macedonia and

*Achaia, but also in every place your faith toward God has gone forth, so that we have no need to say anything.'*
                                        (1 Thessalonians 1:5–8)

By the time that Paul's journeys had taken him as far as Rome, he was able to write of the progress of the gospel up into the former Yugoslav republics:

*'...I will not presume to speak of anything except what Christ has accomplished through me, resulting in the obedience of the Gentiles by word and deed, in the power of signs and wonders, in the power of the Spirit; so that from Jerusalem and round about as far as Illyricum, I have fully preached the gospel of Christ.'*          (Romans 15:18–19)

Descriptions like these give an encouraging account of the spiritual foundations that remain our heritage to rediscover. But at the same time they are indicators of the level of loss that has been the European experience.

## Six Core Decisions

The dissipation of the power of the gospel as it advanced into Europe can in our view be traced to at least six core decisions. While not all were conscious or deliberate in the minds of the leaders, hindsight reveals the increasing distance from the ancient pathways set by the early apostles. We believe they have gradually but steadily led us away from these marvellous foundations and that over the centuries, one after the other, these decisions have set up and solidified into strongholds actually resistant to the original power and impact of the gospel.

## Decision to Divide

The first division of the Church was ratified at the Council of Nicea in 325 AD, which was convened by the converted emperor, Constantine. He had brought the persecution of the Church to an end and was ostensibly concerned for its unity. There were two main topics for discussion, both of which were causing great debate among believers. They were the supposedly heretical teachings of Arius and the date for celebrating Easter. But behind the debate over Easter was a very far-reaching issue. The question was over whether to celebrate the Jewish Passover date, which had huge significance for Jewish believers, or whether to keep the more symbolic date that had grown up in the history of the Gentile Church. But behind it was the even greater issue of whether you could be culturally a Jew and a Christian. In the end the Council ratified an anti-Jewish position following the clearly stated advice of the emperor and confirmed by the assembled bishops. In his letter to the Council Constantine made the position very clear:

'It seems to everyone a most unworthy thing that we should follow the custom of the Jews in the celebration of this most holy solemnity, who, polluted wretches! having stained their hands with a nefarious crime, are justly blinded in their minds. It is fit, therefore, that, rejecting the practice of this people, we should perpetuate to all future ages the celebration of this rite, in a more legitimate order ... Let us then have nothing in common with the most hostile rabble of the Jews. In pursuing this course with a unanimous consent, let us withdraw ourselves ... from that most odious fellowship.'

By ratifying this position the Council officially established an anti-Judaic foundation for the doctrine and practice of the Church and declared that separation from the Jews was the only proper Christian practice. This was a far cry from the New Testament days when Paul was defending the Gentile believers from the Judaizers who attempted to deny Gentiles the freedom to practise their faith without adopting Jewish customs. Now the Jewish roots of the gospel were regarded with contempt and the only way a Jew could be a Christian was by repudiating his or her Jewishness. From the fourth century until the advent of the Messianic congregations at the beginning of the twentieth century it was impossible to be a Jewish Christian. This is massively significant in that the hearts of the children were turning away from their fathers. Until this point the Church embodied difference. The existence of Jewish believers alongside Gentiles safeguarded unity in diversity. It protected both individual believers and varieties of expressions of Church from control, and allowed the body of Christ to express the gospel in a way that honoured and related to the different cultural expressions of the day. The advice of Jesus to the apostle John had been adhered to:

> *'And John ... said, "Master, we saw someone casting out demons in Your name; and we tried to hinder him because he does not follow along with us." But Jesus said to him, "Do not hinder him; for he who is not against you is for you."'*
> (Luke 9:49–50)

But from Nicea on division was to be the order of the day in Europe, with the eventual division of East from West in the separation of the Orthodox Church from the Roman Catholic and then the subdivisions that followed the Reformation and have multiplied until today.

## From Division to Persecution

It was not long before the persecution of the Jews by both Church and State followed this divisive decision. From the fourth century onwards Jews were prohibited from proselytising or marrying Christians, constructing new synagogues or from receiving compensation if existing ones were burnt down. In France during the reign of Charlemagne synagogues were destroyed and worshippers were forced to convert to Christianity at pain of death. The Crusades were as equally aimed at Jews as Moslems, and in their wake Richard 1 (the Lion-Heart) spread anti-Semitic fervour to

Britain. His coronation in 1189 was attended by the burning of the London Jewry, with the loss of thirty lives. In the months following there were attacks on the Jewish community in several places. In Britain, the towns of Kings Lynn, Norwich, Stamford and Lincoln prepared the way for the death by fire and mass suicide of the Jewish people in York in 1190. The notion of the blood-libel, the idea that as the Jews killed Jesus, therefore all Jews were the enemies of Christians, became popular. Britain was the first country to carry out 'the final solution', namely the mass expulsion of Jews. For 600 years from the twelfth to the eighteenth century Jews virtually vanished from Britain. Europe has been justly described as the world's largest Jewish graveyard and it was not just the horror of the twentieth-century Holocaust that earned us that title. Given the biblical exhortation to honour our parents and the link to long life and blessing, it is hardly surprising that this treatment of our spiritual fathers has impeded the progress of the gospel. Add to it the apostle Paul's exhortations to the Romans on the Jews' behalf, such as the following, and it is clear just how far from the gospel path we have strayed:

> *'I am telling the truth, I am not lying, my conscience bearing me witness in the Holy Spirit, that I have great sorrow and unceasing grief in my heart. For I could wish that I myself were accursed, separated from Christ for the sake of my brethren, my kinsmen according to the flesh, who are Israelites, to whom belongs the adoption as sons and the glory and the covenants and the giving of the Law and the temple service and the promises, whose are the fathers, and from whom is the Christ according to the flesh, who is over all, God blessed forever.'* (Romans 9:1–5)

## The Nature of Authority

Following the development of division and the acceptance of persecution as a church practice, power-based conflict became the norm for dealing with differences in church life.

What was really happening was all part of a subtle but at times virtually total exchange of spiritual for secular authority. As we have already seen, this first became obvious with the conversion of the Roman emperor Constantine in the early fourth century. Instead of the Church being the agent of the apostolic invasion of the good news of the Kingdom of God and its values and lifestyle flowing from the preaching of Jesus and the fellowship of the Holy Spirit, it became the agent of the State and the means of legitimating its power and authority by means of 'correct', universally accepted and enforced religious rules and customs. This was no minor departure from gospel principles. The problem was that the state authorities in Europe largely flowed out from the empires of Greece and Rome which biblical prophecy linked inextricably to the ancient powers of Babylon and Assyria. These in turn were the enemies of God's Kingdom in its early development and history. When the prophet Daniel was told by the Archangel Gabriel that his prayers were heard, his desired answer was that all *'the sovereignty, the dominion, and the greatness of all the kingdoms under the whole heaven will be given to the people of the saints of the Highest One; His kingdom will be an everlasting kingdom, and all the dominions will serve and obey Him'* (Daniel 7:27–28). The reason for the delay in his answer was the battle between the angelic forces and the princes of Greece and Persia (Daniel 10:13, 20). But well before the end of the first half of Europe's second-day mission task, the spirit and authority of those enemies of the Kingdom of God had invaded the Church at the highest levels. As we have seen from Daniel's experience, the Scriptures understood the powers of empire as being invested in spiritual forces, not just earthly authorities. The terrible implication of this is that the exchange of the spiritual authority of the Church for the secular was actually welcoming demonic powers into authority in the Church.

The prophecy of Zechariah, quoted by Jesus more than any other book, deals with the nature of these spiritual powers of empire. Chapter 4 of the book is well known and much quoted as summarising the heart of the way the Kingdom of

God works and comes in a place. It's *'"not by might nor by power, but by My Spirit," says the Lord of Hosts'* (v. 6). Chapter 5 is much less well known, yet just as simply, but in contrast to the previous chapter, it gives the basis of the way the enemy's kingdom gets established. Two female spirits carry an ephah, a huge covered measuring bowl. Within the bowl is 'wickedness', the spirit of imperial civilisations. The feminine in Scripture alludes to the being fruitful, settling, civilising role, good or bad, but in this case clearly bad. There are two specific feminine spirit beings identified in the Scripture as having a key role in empires against the Kingdom of God. The first is Jezebel, an actual Sidonian princess who marries into the royal house of Israel's northern kingdom and who comes to represent spiritual authority against God's plans for His people.[1] She re-emerges as a spiritual power again in New Testament times standing against the work of the Kingdom of God in the European gateway city of Thyatira in what is now Turkey.[2] We will look at the significance of all seven churches as gateways into Europe in the last chapter. It is our view that the Jezebel spirit is one of these two spirits that sustain the authority of the world's empires. The main traits of this spirit in Scripture are idolatry, sexual immorality, false prophecy, antagonism to true prophecy, control, disinheritance and murder.[3] The second spirit is the Queen of Heaven. Her main characteristics are enticement to idolatrous worship and occult practices, and the sacrifice of children, particularly the sacrifice of sons to the imperial ideal in war. In the exchange of the spiritual authority of the Kingdom of God for the secular authority of the State, the Church in Europe allowed these spirit powers to invade the Church and begin to set up the culture of the enemy's empire right inside the Church. For example, in the main events of the Reformation in England, leading to the establishing of the Church of England, Henry VIII was trying to justify his sexual immorality, and secure his control of the kingdom against other competing powers within Europe. In the process he used disinheritance and murder to remove his opponents, the monasteries and even his wives. Throughout the whole

Reformation period and until the present day the Jezebel spirit has been firmly established within many Protestant Churches.

Before the coming of the gospel to Europe the Queen of Heaven was worshipped in many places under many guises. Some were from outside Europe but had become entrenched in places of influence through the trade of empire. She was the pagan goddess Sibyl, Diana of the Ephesians, Isis of the Egyptians, Artemis of the Greeks and Minerva of the Romans. When the Romans invaded Britain they minted a coin to commemorate the conquest. Under the portrait of Minerva, their goddess of war, was the inscription 'Britannia'. This is the earliest known record of Britannia, which leads us to conclude that Britannia of the British is also a manifestation of the Queen of Heaven. With the conversion of Constantine and the adoption of Christianity as the religion of the empire, the Queen of Heaven invaded the Roman Church. The proper honour and recognition afforded to Mary along-side the apostles was demonically invaded and transformed into the worship of the Queen of Heaven in the guise of a false Mary. Together with the invasion of Protestantism by the Jezebel spirit, the Church in Europe gave welcome to the two powers who hold together the enemy's false empire. Of course it is an over-simplification to limit the Queen of Heaven to the Roman Church and Jezebel to the Protestants. Both are within each. The Queen of Heaven is particularly strong within some branches of Anglicanism. Thus the Church in Europe became in part a vehicle for the spirit of wickedness, and as well as carrying the good seed of the Kingdom of God, mixed it with the very powers of empire that it was designed to overcome and destroy! Hardly surprising, we conclude, that the gospel took so much time to get out to the ends of the earth.

## The Reformation: A Bridge Not Far Enough

From Constantine and the Council of Nicea onwards, European culture developed around a Church–State axis where what sociologists call the legitimating power of religion dominated over the radical gospel of the Kingdom of God. This had a number of crucial effects. To begin with those elements of the gospel that reinforced the secular power of the government of the day were used against the expression of the gospel that allowed for the invasion of the Kingdom of God into the hearts of men and women. This was in part deliberate, and in part the unconscious consequence of theological confusion. Nor did it mean that aspects of the gospel that preserved biblical, Holy Spirit Christianity were absent from the Roman or Orthodox Churches. But the tendency to conservatism and traditionalism that is necessary to uphold the status quo of the social order kept the liturgy in Latin and the Scriptures from ordinary people. Those with the openness of heart and mind and sufficient education to uncover the truth and become radical leaders were frequently persecuted, outlawed, or killed as traitors and enemies of state. The key issue for many of them was the discovery that there are no second-generation Christians and that membership of the Church comes by new birth, not by being born in a particular nation or state, despite the existence of a state Church. Generally they asserted that the traditional form of Christian initiation in state church contexts, infant baptism, was not a biblical practice. Their tendency was to baptise adult believers on personal confession of faith. This was regarded as re-baptism by the state church authorities, and as such was rightly seen as a rejection of state Christianity. The radicals often became known as Ana-baptists, those who baptise people again.

Reformers like these were relatively commonplace throughout the years following Constantine, through the division into the Roman Catholic and Eastern Orthodox Churches, right up to the Reformation and of course on to the present day. Europe owes these people a huge debt of gratitude both for the gradual groundswell of biblical vision that led up to the Reformation and for the subsequent development of freedoms of speech, democracy and social justice which became for significant seasons more or less the norm in

Europe in parts of the nineteenth and twentieth centuries. Radicals like these, known as Paulicians and Bogomils were numerous in Armenia, Turkey, Bulgaria and Bosnia. They were known as Albigenses in France, Waldenses in Italy and Hussites in Bohemia. Both exciting and carefully researched accounts of the history of these radicals can be found in E.H. Broadbent's book *The Pilgrim Church* (Pickering and Inglis, 1946). It is these revival movements, together with those within the Roman Catholic and Orthodox Churches which were often subsumed into monastic movements within the institutional Church, that produced the sense of burnt ground across Europe that John Mulinde and others refer to and we shall examine in more detail later.

With the Reformation, this core understanding of the need for individual conversion and the recovery of the theology of justification by faith which undergirded it, burst out upon Europe. While we refuse to deny that the older state Churches of Rome and Constantinople still carried genuine gospel grace and anointing, it is clear from subsequent history that the Reformation represented the revelatory reform that led to the subsequent breakout of the gospel of the Kingdom of God to the ends of the earth. While reformation was already a process, Martin Luther's act of courage in nailing his theses to the door of Wittenburg Cathedral was the prophetic crisis that released the gospel in Europe towards the dawn of the third day that is now upon us. Yet despite this breakthrough the Reformation carried with it the seeds of a further corruption even more subtle than the social legitimation of state Christianity which had covered such essential truths of the gospel. Put simply, the Reformation uncovered the truths of personal salvation but never really dealt with the issue of the sell-out of spiritual authority for the so-called secular or state authority. The implications of this were absolutely devastating. We have already noted that state church authority was not really secular at all. Rather it represented the invasion of the ancient spiritual powers of empire that the states of Europe had inherited from years of domination by the empires of

Greece and Rome, themselves the inheritors of the imperial spirits of the empires of Egypt, Assyria and Babylon that they had swallowed up. In fact, it was the spirit and mindset of Greece in particular that had formed the idea of the secular State and the subordination of religion to the state powers. The biblical, Hebrew paradigm never divides the so-called secular from the spiritual and has a whole world-view in which all of life and society, including the authority of the State, is submitted to the authority and revelation of God. By the time of the Reformation, the Church in Europe needed corporate exorcism and a complete paradigm shift into a biblical mindset of the nature and function of true spiritual authority. Tragically this is precisely what failed to happen. Luther ultimately panicked at the way the ordinary peasants following him began to revolt against the state authorities. Excommunicated from the Roman Church and seemingly faced with the choice of revolution or state authority he hid behind the newly emerging princes and their states, resulting inevitably in the formation of the new, now Protestant state Churches of northern Europe. Calvin, on the other hand, equally disastrously made a brave attempt to create a Hebrew theocracy in Geneva but without understanding spiritual authority in the light of the incarnation.

## The Enlightenment, Humanism and Confusion!

There are important things we need to learn from this which will be our subject in later chapters. For the moment we simply need to understand what happened next. It all led to great new freedom for the individual in both thought and expression, a freedom increasingly unhindered by the conservative, legitimating power of the old Roman and Orthodox forms of state Christianity. A new radicalism in thought, art and politics which we now call the Enlightenment, spread throughout the new courts of Europe. While it created wonderful intellectual and increasing political space for the spread of a much more biblical Christianity, the European Church failed to break its unholy submission to the State with its Greek mindset and demonisation by ancient imperial spirits. This led to the development of Humanism and to what the apostle Paul calls in the book of Romans the worship of *'the creature rather than the Creator'* (1:25). Eventually Humanism became the new threat to biblical Holy Spirit Christianity as the new form of social legitimation. In its variant forms of Socialism and Capitalism, Humanism increasingly either vied for or shared power with both the old and new state Churches. One of the major effects of the release of Humanism within Europe was to give a whole new lease of life and shape to the imperial spirit. Up until the Reformation and Enlightenment this had mainly been contained within the confines of so-called Christendom. But now the spirit of enterprise and adventure thrust explorers and buccaneers out to the boundaries of the known world and beyond. New empires spread out from both the old Roman Catholic and new Protestant states aggressively colonising as they went. This gave room for a genuine missionary impetus to spread out from the Roman Catholic Church while the new release and understanding of the gospel manifest by the Reformation gave rise to a new worldwide missionary vision that at last began also to thrust biblical Holy Spirit Christianity to the uttermost parts of the earth.

Yet the terrible failure of the European Church to complete the Reformation by exorcising the imperial spirits and changing the falsely divided Greek mindset of secular and spiritual authority led inevitably to a dreadful confusion of the aims of mission and empire. In some cases this confusion was there in the colonisers and missionaries themselves. At other times it existed in the perception of those people groups and nations on the receiving end of empire and mission. Whatever the case the result was a mixture of blessing and oppressing spreading out from Europe all around the earth throughout the last 400 years. The name and reputation of Europe is confused and tarnished by a catalogue of oppressive and wounding colonial initiatives throughout the world. This was despite the many positive gifts that the gospel brought to and through Europe in its long history, many of which were deposited throughout the earth during the colonial process. Those nations whose empires were the perpetrators of this confusion, nations such as Spain, Portugal, France, Italy, Germany, Russia and more than any other Great Britain, need to uncover and repent for the sins of this era in particular. The book which Brian Mills and Roger wrote together, *The Sins of the Fathers* (Sovereign World, 1999) gives the British perspective.

## Demonic Developments

One of the most terrible consequences of the exchange of the true authority of the Kingdom of God for the authority of the State was the attempt to deal with the twelfth-century Moslem threat to the 'Christian' states of Europe by means of the violence of the Crusades. The so-called final victory of the First Crusade with the massacre of Jews and Moslems alike in Jerusalem left the Knights of the Temple of Solomon, better known as the Knights Templar, in the main position of power in Jerusalem. Founded on the site of Solomon's temple in 1118, from which they take their name, they filled the desperate need of a standing army to continue the military defence of the Holy Land. They soon grew in numbers, wealth and political power, and although they eventually lost control of Jerusalem in 1187, they managed to hold on to a narrow strip of territory along the Mediterranean coast. Eventually interest in sending money and men to help support the Templars waned among the European governments and in 1297 they were defeated by the Sultan of Egypt and moved their base to Cyprus in the vain hope of drumming up new support for another crusade to liberate the Holy Land. By this time, however, they had used the past financial support to establish a major banking operation and many European states, not least France, were seriously indebted to them. When the threat of English domination had been removed by the death of Edward I of England, King Philip IV of France, with the support of Pope Clement V, used the opportunity to bring the Templar's ageing Grand Master to France. Leading him to believe that he was about to support him in a new crusade, the king deceived him until at dawn on Friday 13 October 1307 every Templar in France was arrested and put in chains and tortured by order of the Pope, and the Templars were formally excommunicated from the Roman Catholic Church. While the decree to arrest them finally followed them into England, the English king delayed it, and in Scotland it was never even published. The result was that England and especially Scotland became the seedbed for the most successful and ultimately all-pervading secret society in the history of the world, the Freemasons. In his carefully researched book, *Born in Blood* (M. Evans & Co., 1989), John J. Robinson concludes,

> 'There remained no reasonable doubt in my mind that the original concept of the secret society that came to call itself Freemasonry had been born as a society of mutual protection among fugitive Templars and their associates in Britain, men who had gone underground to escape the imprisonment and torture that had been ordered for them by Pope Clement V.'

The task of tracing the genesis of a secret society like the Masons is a difficult one, and the dangers of becoming lost in the labyrinths of conspiracy theories very real. However a proper understanding of the role of Freemasons in the colonial process is vital to uncovering and repenting for the depth and strength of the imperial spirit that succeeded in bringing Europe to the spiritual captivity that resulted and climaxed in the First World War, a captivity which is only now giving place to a new opportunity for full revival and restoration. The fact that the development of Freemasonry was rooted in the defence of Christendom but yet they were rejected by the very Church–State axis of power that upheld it, led to their development as an alternative religious power base for upholding and promoting imperial civilisation. At the highest levels of initiation they re-enacted Haggai the prophet, Joshua the high priest and Zerubbabel the king receiving the restored Kingdom of God from the Ancient of Days. They had become, as they saw it, the rightful heirs of the city and temple that they had defended and of the empires of Christendom that they represented. But it was no longer the Kingdom of God. Significantly, Masons can be sworn in by the name of Jahweh, Allah and Bramah, but not Jesus Christ. The absence of allegiance to Jesus gave full place to the spiritual powers of empire that had begun to invade the Church and the violence that the Crusades expressed. Now Freemasonry sought out the idolatrous spiritual imagery and artefacts of the ancient empires. Its temples were unashamedly wombs and its memorial obelisks phalluses. The lives of its sons laid down in defence of empire became the honoured seed offered to the Queen of Heaven. A huge amount of serious research remains to be done on this subject but enough is apparent to conclude that by the nineteenth century they were established everywhere the British empire went, providing social support and legitimacy for the colonial enterprise, sometimes as an alternative to the Anglican and other Protestant Churches, sometimes alongside or within them.

## The War: The Climax of European History

While they are not alone to be blamed for the competitive imperial wars of the period, they provided a great deal of the leadership and carry major responsibility for the great colonial and imperial climax that was the First World War. We see this war, alongside many non-Christian historians, as the defining moment in European history. Coming at the time when the European day of world mission was at last coming to its zenith, when a new Pentecostal outpouring in Wales was poised and ready to flood Europe again with revival fire, when the two greatest missionary sending nations were Britain and Germany, it represented the choice of the empires of men over the Kingdom of God and the authority of the spirits of empire over the authority of God's

Holy Spirit. The First World War poet Wilfred Owen captured the full significance of the day in his poem, 'The parable of the old man and the young':

> So Abram rose, and clave the wood, and went,
> And took the fire with him, and a knife.
> And as they sojourned both of them together,
> Isaac the first-born spake and said, My Father,
> Behold the preparations, fire and iron,
> But where the lamb, for this burnt-offering?
> Then Abram bound the youth with belts and straps,
> And builded parapets and trenches there,
> And stretched forth the knife to slay his son.
> When lo! An Angel called him out of heaven,
> Saying, Lay not thy hand upon the lad,
> Neither do anything to him, thy son.
> Behold! Caught in a thicket by its horns,
> A Ram. Offer the Ram of Pride instead.
>
> But the old man would not so, but slew his son
> And half the seed of Europe, one by one.[4]

## Ongoing Ritual

In 2 Kings 3:26–27 the Scriptures describe the action of the King of Moab who, when he saw that he was losing the battle against the kings of Israel, sacrificed his own son on the wall. In so doing he accessed such spiritual power against the people of God that they departed and went to their own land. The choice of the fathers of Europe to sacrifice their own sons on the altars of their pride of empire similarly released demonic power against the Kingdom and the people of God in Europe. In the wound of Germany's defeat, as we all know, there grew up in Hitler an expression of the European imperial spirit that murdered six million Jews. But even today the honoured seed of the sons of Europe that helped defeat him is being accessed along with those from the First World War in shrines to the dead, frequently

constructed by Freemasons, which are central to the architecture and spiritual shape of thousands of towns, cities and
villages throughout many parts of Europe and the world.
Traditional rituals of remembrance, albeit out of a genuine
desire to remember dead relatives and real heroism, together
with ongoing occult practices keep alive the terrible consequences of the wrong decisions of the fathers of Europe.
Today we are faced with a continent ruled increasingly by
state Humanism, in which the spirits of empire seem to have
abated, but they have not gone away. In the East where
Humanism in its Socialist form has broken up, new nation-
alist spirits are rising, but popular belief has it that the
Humanism of the West will eventually bring new enlightenment and peace. However, the biblical data remind us that
the sexual and occult practices now normalised in western
humanistic culture are evidence of the presence of the worst
forms of imperial spirits in history. In this context the people
and the Kingdom of God have experienced nearly a hundred
years of net loss in Europe. This is in no way to despise
the extraordinary people that God has gifted to the body, the
blessings, missionary enterprises, answered prayers, revelations, new movements and the like. But all has been in the
context of a terrible captivity – like the Israelites in Babylon.
The question is how the European Church has fared in this
captivity time and if, as we are convinced, the captivity is
coming to an end, what needs to happen next? This is the
subject of our next chapter.

## Notes

1. See 1 Kings 16:31; 19:1–2; 21:1–16
2. See Revelation 2:20–23
3. See Jeremiah 7:17–18; 44:16–19
4. Wilfred Owen: *War Poems*, Jon Stallworthy (Editor), Chatto and
   Windus, London, 1994

## Chapter 3

# The End of the Captivity?

If such an historical overview is anywhere near an accurate assessment of the state of European faith, we should well begin this chapter in the depths of Despond! Despite the undoubted glory and power of the gospel, it has still come to this? Where can we find hope for restoration, and if possible redemption? It could well be right to talk in terms of impossibility. The book of Hebrews encourages us to be realistic about the size of the task,

> *'For in the case of those who have once been enlightened and have tasted of the heavenly gift ... and then have fallen away, it is impossible to renew them again to repentance.'*
> (Hebrews 6:4, 6)

It has to be faced that to restore the European peoples to a vibrant experience of living faith and power is as impossible as a virgin conceiving a child. It requires that the God of all mercy and compassion revive again, indeed resurrect, a desperate people.

## A Quickening?

There is something about the passing of time that God wrote into the human context to catch our attention. Towards the end of the nineteenth century, then, like so recently, the approaching turning of the century evoked a sense of significant time passing. It seemed to cause a stirring among many streams of God's people who gathered in conferences, like the Edinburgh conference on world evangelisation in 1900, to focus and strategise towards the goal of world evangelisation, which, according to the Lord's words, must be accomplished before the end of all things. It was like the early flutterings in the womb of a new child, the quickening. One could wonder whether it was this stirring, this unity and strategic planning, that was seen and answered by God in the outpourings in Wales and Los Angeles. These, as we have considered, were then completely contested by the twentieth-century's two desperate world wars. Yet a similar surging in the hearts of God's people began to be expressed at the approach of the turning of the millennium. This really focused our longings and our goals! What could we offer Jesus for His 2000th birthday? How could a Church of such longevity show itself to be mature and responsible enough for such a time as this? It is invidious to cut into any particular point of history to begin to plot a developmental process, but we believe we can map the outline of a process which began with another of God's marvellous multi-layered initiatives to prepare us for a change of 'millennial' significance. The themes or layers of this move that we will draw attention to could be summed up by the following key words: humility, intercession, intervention, transition and perseverance.

## Prophetic Challenge

In the mid 1980s a surge of interest in and experience of prophetic ministry hit the western Church. There is no doubt that various streams of the Church had always practised the prophetic ministry and others had certainly held a theology that would allow for such practice. But perhaps with the growth of world travel and Internet communication, the full emergence into the public arena of the 'Kansas city prophets' and their embrace by John Wimber and the Vineyard movement was, in our view, a key moment. We will consider in a later chapter the theological position of times and seasons when the prophetic ministry comes into an ascendancy, when one comes 'in the spirit and power of Elijah', but for a pragmatic overview we draw attention to the end of the millennium approaching and the impact of a generally accessible prophetic ministry coalescing. Other names could be quoted here, such as the impact of Jean Darnall in the British context, but the phenomenon in itself is important. It certainly kindled hope and excitement as well as being fundamentally provoking! It climaxed for us in Britain with the word from Paul Cain that revival would break out in London in 1988. So sure were he and John Wimber that this was from the Lord, that they organised a large conference in the Docklands arena in October of that year, and many Americans who had heard the word flew in at the same time, so as not to miss what God was about to do in Europe. It coincided with other words concerning the new partnership of Germany and England in this revival, and God putting His footprints in both London and Berlin.

How does one assess the validity of such a word? It was a stirring conference. Many were energised to hope, pray and rise in their level of expectation like never before. That 'nothing more' than that transpired at the time caused some to assess this word as false prophecy. Where was the great harvest promised? With hindsight (that great revealer of mysteries), if we reconsider the impossibility of the task given the European context, we believe God began an enormously significant work at that time. There was so much groundwork to be done, so much preparation of the Church to be addressed, before the harvest could be gathered. Indeed, it has been argued that 'revival' should always refer to the Church rather than a great ingathering, as it connotes reactivating something that was alive. So the prophetic words began to have a provoking effect. Isn't that biblical? Hope is stirred and the questions are asked. The answers are not always what we want or expect to hear at first. Some of the subsequent prophetic insights were particularly challenging for those of us engaged in the most recently radical move of God, the British Charismatic movement.

When Paul Cain went on to ask whether the Charismatic movement might have been Ishmael rather than Isaac, many were deeply offended. When prophets from Brazil of whom we had never heard wrote with warnings that the leaders in London were not listening to what God wanted to say, we discounted them as untested, untried ministries.

But new hope had been kindled and, despite disappointment, it wouldn't go away! In fact, disappointment seemed to have an interesting effect. We began to look from a different perspective and to see a little more honestly. We had been in a season of extremely successful church planting. Since the early 1980s, God had led many new and established churches to think in terms of planting new congregations, and many had seen the fruit of such vision. However, as we lifted our eyes at this time, expecting and hoping to see a great harvest, what we did see was a new landscape. Churches were indeed growing, some quite significantly. We had been part of the development of one congregation of 400 people growing into a multi-congregational grouping of 2000 people in a few short years. But lifting our eyes from the immediate activity and blessing of that to the nation showed a different story. For all the church growth, London was worse than ever. For all the new energy and activity in the Church across the land, the nation itself was more pagan, more corrupt and more overtly unclean than for many a long year. We were challenged by the words of Jesus that if the signs done in His ministry had been done in Sodom and Gomorrah then they would have repented. But here was London more like Sodom and Gomorrah than ever in its history. Where was the ministry that would cause this great city to repent? So the full effect of the prophetic words was finally to bring us to a humbling desperation. Thank God! How else would revival, in its truly biblical form, be patterned?

## Prayer for Europe and Prayer in Europe!

At the same time we in Europe became aware of the intercession movement rising across the world that we referred to earlier. By the 1980s many had heard of the establishment of 'prayer mountains' in Korea. The largest church in the world was now established and still growing in Seoul. It seemed to have been born out of the suffering of Yonggi Cho and his long years of lying sick that he and his mother-in-law had invested in prayer. Now the harvest of that planting was evident. And not just in that church! Right across the country, churches were growing and manifesting extra-ordinary discipline and effectiveness in prayer. It seems to us that this is the true fruit and redemptive purpose of the Korean revival. Its timing and revelation into the world church scene was perfect. For us in the West it was an extraordinary sight. The exhortation 'let us pray' had new meaning since this really was corporate prayer! In the most gentle and organised way, thousands of people could be engaged in the work of effective, aggressive, vocal prayer together. On the back of this mobilisation, thousands would also give sacrificial personal time to ascend mountains (yes, there was more than one), lock themselves in small, basic cells, fast and beseech God for their nation and indeed the nations of the world. Then news began to arrive of other nations likewise engaged in such fervent, corporate prayer. We now know of millions of Christians from the nations of South America and Africa as well as Asia where prayer was vibrant, sacrificial and, most wonderfully of all, focused on Europe. God, while speaking into Europe and beginning to bring us to our knees, was also stirring vast prayer **for** us among the nations.

So finally, in Europe also, prayer began to appear higher on the agenda. Prayer movements, often initiated by women such as Lydia and Aglow, had already been functioning and only time will tell how great a debt of gratitude we owe them for where they had stood in the gap for a relative prayerlessness in local church. Now, however, this burden began to be experienced right across the church body. We remember the exercise of so many teachers and preachers around that time, since it was also happening to us. We seemed only to be able to teach on prayer! Then there was the resurgence of reading the great books of the apostles of prayer. There was teaching, discussion and disagreement over different forms of prayer from contemplation to high praise to spiritual warfare. Many agreed to differ in a new atmosphere where increasingly the Church was engaging in much more practice of the lost art! Gaining momentum, the Church took to the streets with worship via March for Jesus, and a prayer and worship movement spread right out across the globe climaxing in 'A Day to Change the World' when, from the rising of the sun to the setting, the Lord's name was honoured and praised on the streets of hundreds of nations! Now this was a marvellous sign and wonder! Together, yes together, Church of all shape, size and ecclesiology began to be manifest as one body, agreed in prayer and praise for the goodness of God and His concern for our cities and nations. The need and burden for prayer in all its forms was beginning to impact European church life.

The consequent changing climate of spiritual vision from depression to rising hope in England in the early 1990s was amply demonstrated in the Challenge 2000 goals set by leaders of more than thirty denominations and streams who met together in Birmingham in 1992. That such a gathering could take place at all was a sign. That they could find agreement and a rising tide of faith that together, across more than thirty denominations or streams of churches, these leaders could make an agreement to see 20,000 new churches planted by the year 2000 was awesome. It could mean only one thing. Humanly, the goals were outrageous. That we could hope and even believe for them, let alone strategise towards them, was nothing short of miraculous. Only true revival could achieve them. This was either fool-hardy in the extreme, or the kind of visionary leadership that God would have to honour somehow. As Roger prayed at a leaders' gathering following this conference, the Lord granted him the most extraordinary open vision. He saw an ox. It was rising from the ground in great strength and purpose and had a life and energy that seemed to be penetrating into his own inner being. Now this was worrying!

Should he allow this? What did it mean? Again, as began to happen so many times in this season of longing and searching, there was only God to enquire of. His answer was the scripture:

> '*As the first-born of his ox, majesty is his,*
> *And His horns are the horns of the wild ox;*
> *With them he shall push the peoples,*
> *all at once, to the ends of the earth.*'

(Deuteronomy 33:17)

Whatever else was happening, something was rising in Britain that would have the strength and purpose of the blessing of Joseph and its effect would be to bring in the fullness of the great commission. The peoples of the earth must hear. Energy, strength and clear missionary mandate have been called forth from these islands before. More will be said about the relevance of the Joseph imagery. But what of majesty? Referred to by some as the redemptive gift of Britain, this gift is bittersweet. Could God really intend to reawaken and renew a leadership gift in these lands that would model on earth the true servant leadership of our Lord Jesus? What would be necessary to undo the abuse of this gift in the past? What might have worried us more at the time, had we noticed it then, was the little word 'wild'.

A little known message by Ian Andrews, a healing evangelist from Somerset in Britain, might have better prepared us. Finding himself in Minneapolis at a time when the snow was ankle deep, unbeknown to him Ian was about to fulfil another prophetic word. Kept there by God's intention, Ian experienced angelic visitations which brought a revelation word to that area back in 1993. It referred to 'God wanting His Church back' and was perhaps a forerunner word about the necessary 'wildness' that was about to break on the Church. We remember the power manifestations that went with the word even when Ian reported it back in England, but as with many forerunner words, it was seeded but we had to wait for the fruit.

## Intervention: What Could It Mean?

The Holy Spirit's visitation in Toronto in January 1994 and less well reported but simultaneous phenomena in many parts of Europe burst into the church consciousness and fulfilled the word 'wild'! Again we thank God for hindsight! We believe it has to be said that, despite some people's reservations, the overall impact of the Toronto phenomenon was faith building and church changing. It was an intervention. Now, after these years, we do not find many people who disagree with that opinion. Even where parts of the Church have decided that the experiences associated with what came to be known as the 'Toronto Blessing' did not bless them, they do agree that the overall impact in the Church at large is that people are more hopeful than they were before. Many may have come to the opinion that it may have got a little out of hand, it may have had fleshly responses mixed in with it, but that at some level it was and is an intervention from God. Personally we were and are thrilled with how God moved into and through our lives in a new and greater way, and those of many of our friends and colleagues. We have examined the testimony of many touched by the flow of life from the wells that sprang up in many places during this season and believe it truly manifests really good fruit. But we recognise that it was wild! We love the allusion in C.S. Lewis' *Narnia Chronicles* when the children have to agree that 'Aslan is not a **tame** lion!' In the face of centuries when the Church has inevitably solidified, calcified into heavyweight structures and mindsets, wouldn't God have to do a 'strange act'?

So what, now, could be said about the impact? 'It offended the mind to reveal the spirit' was a description used often of some of the experiences. They seemed to make little or no sense to the rational questions. We remember one evening when laughter was breaking out all around an auditorium as the Lord seemed to be touching people and healing depression and coldness. We went home, still light-hearted and somewhat dizzy. The television news that evening was all about the atrocities in Rwanda where genocide of the worst kind was running riot. Rwanda! The name was synonymous with a marvellous move of God in living memory. How can we be laughing, sometimes uncontrollably, when such evil is rampant? How selfish, how trivial is that? But those questions seemed so similar in spirit to the one Judas asked concerning the alabaster vial and the pouring out (wasting, as some would call it) of the precious oil. The wicked do prosper. The poor will always be with us. Do we not therefore need **more** of the conscious presence of God to be effective? In that context, do we not need God to work on our emotions, thoughts, ambitions, softening them up to be able to care in a truer, deeper and more lasting way? These are only some suggestions to assess some of the pragmatic fruit of those early experiences. Many we know of nowadays would testify to being more compassionate out of love, rather than out of duty or persuasion. They function out of healed experience rather than just out of mental assent. But at a more philosophical level and in the overall framework of this book, we believe that such a move of God might well make sense (which we also believe in!) as the antidote to post-Enlightenment idolatry. Where we have as European peoples so esteemed our ability to understand and explain everything, perhaps a new humility is required to recognise that God might want to have fun with little children as well as deep and meaningful conversation with the sage. Perhaps in the light of eternity, we are not quite so mature and wise as we once thought and to 'become like little children' may give us fresh access to entering the Kingdom of God rather than merely teaching about it. It re-emphasised an experience of a love for God to counter the intellectual pride of Humanism.

Another significant emphasis of this move was that it was corporate in its effects. Groups of people were affected together. Again and again in the times of ministry when the Holy Spirit would begin to move in the room, there would be a clear connection among certain individuals which the Holy Spirit seemed to recognise and acknowledge. Indeed, sometimes only He seemed to know of the connection! Very often it was to do with people groups. When all the English were called forward on one evening in Toronto where we were privileged to be, the power of God broke out completely without any human agency or direction as we all fell to the floor spontaneously. All were amazed and those watching noted at the time that God must be about to do a new thing in these little islands! But it seemed He had other 'favourites' too, and we bless the generous hearts of our Canadian friends who, time and time again, rejoiced at the marvellous grace that seemed to fall heavily on the different national groups from Europe. Then different generational groupings seemed to be identified by the Lord. Something was going on of a corporate nature, which was difficult at first for us Europeans to understand. Again from around the world we had models and encouragement to think more corporately, to identify roots and communities to which we belonged in our past and present, and from there we were on a remarkable journey. Some of our corporate identity was so polluted that the guilt would cripple us without a growing understanding of standing in the gap for the sins of our fathers. But some is so blessed that we would be foolish not to draw up the wells of grace which are our inheritance! We feel that this aspect of God's intervention is one of the key markers of a new season for us in Europe. The healing and significance of our historical links and identities is paramount for God at this time in the face of increasing moves in the natural, or even demonic, realms to unite our nations. If they are truly built and restored in the Holy Spirit and under His direction, this reality will take precedence over any false or potentially oppressive structure planned elsewhere!

We want to honour one further aspect of this intervention and make some suggestions at interpretation. We believe it could be argued that this move of God itself patterned the process that God was taking His whole Church through at the time. We know of the personal humility and hunger of John and Carol Arnott who became known (named as such by others) as the figureheads of this move. They had themselves become so hungry for more of God that they had cleared their lives of anything but that seeking. Every morning was given to their calling on God together for more of His presence and intercession for more breakthrough for those who don't yet know Him. They were unknown and unsung. Their very names carry the significance of the move, that God was going to use the things that 'are not' to bring to nothing the things that are. No one more appropriately lives up to their names. This move was and is not about the powerful and famous, but about the humble and seeking. It is about fame and glory for no one but the Lord. It connotes a grassroots move of ordinary people becoming an extra-ordinary body.

But interestingly enough, it has been extraordinarily difficult for anyone to begin to make such statements as to the **meaning** of what God might be purposing through this intervention. Because the phenomena that marked this move were so, let's say again, wild, there was a great resistance to interpreting them. They were called 'extra-biblical' and therefore in some sense, meaningless, or irrelevant to, or of a different order than reasoned explanation. They could perhaps be received as ecstatic, in the same way as 'other tongues', but not interpreted. Now, if they were of the same order as ecstatic tongues or prophecy (and we believe they are at least that), are we not in fact biblically mandated to interpret them? It may be that as with tongue speaking, some utterances or manifestations are more for personal worship and expression to God, and therefore left to the individual to learn from, but surely some actually require a corporate attempt at discernment. After due reflection, it seems to us that as well as the previous comments we have made, the following interpretations can also be drawn. A serious biblical examination of some of the manifestations that were evident particularly in the early stages of this visitation is highly revealing. Descriptions of the phenomena of shaking, falling down and speechlessness can frequently be traced to the visitation of angels. Take Daniel, for example. He groaned and fell down as all strength left him. He was speechless with fear and wonder. He also began to understand his relationship with his people and his people's history. Reports of angelic visitations were not uncommon during this present move of God. It seems to be complementary to the revelation of the demonic sphere and activity more commonly associated with the earlier Pentecostal and Charismatic outpourings. But further, the appearance of angels (and the ecstatic responses) seems biblically to be associated with times of transition when God is raising up somebody (indeed, a body) to bring about the restoration of His Kingdom purposes, as with Daniel, Ezekiel, or in the New Testament, Zechariah. The sign of laughter and angels come together most gloriously with the conception of the child of the promise, when Sarah laughed (see Genesis 18). She was embarrassed enough by the irrationality of it to deny that she laughed, but none the less she was overcome with the very presence of the spiritual promise as the angels carried it, and receive it she did! Faith for the restoration of European Christianity has been kindled by this intervention and we are only really mad if we don't lay hold of it with all our might!

Finally, in the context of our corporate European history and the development of the Jezebelic strongholds we have already referred to, we may in fact have confirmation of them by some of our very responses to these things. The first Jezebel always resisted the prophetic and threatened it at every point. If, as we believe, this whole initiative of God has been part of a prophetic season, birthed in the prophetic and prayed into being by prophetic intercession, would it not inevitably draw out angry resistance and opposition? But at this point, let's be very careful not to point the finger and call our friends or members of our own body 'Jezebelic', but check our own fears, our own internal struggles, our own cultural and historical paradigm that might resist the 'wildness' of God and His right to do a new thing in a new season of restoration. Do not our nations need something this different and this big? Let's stand in the gap and cry 'mercy!' as the season changes.

## Transition Time

The next theme during this time was a major re-positioning. The word 'transition' was on everybody's lips. Individually, which was the way we were all trained to process our experience then, many found during the early to mid 1990s that they changed jobs or moved house. We have only anecdotal evidence, but we do have a great deal of it! As we taught and listened during this time, the Lord had given Sue a sense of five waves (the number of grace) which, for the purpose of easier remembering, began (with the occasional tweak!) with 'p': poverty (humility), petition (intercession), out-pouring (intervention), positioning and perseverance. During this time, we offered it as an interpretative tool for some of our corporate experiences and it struck chord after chord. There is no doubt at all that a far greater than average incidence of house or job moving was happening in the mid 1990s. Alongside this, in Britain at least, our church relationships were also undergoing transition and reshaping. Because of house or city moving, many found themselves in new local congregations. Others suffered at the time from the need to change without a geographical move, either with or without their own personal choices of where to belong! It was frequently traumatic and demanding, but what we were scenting was the necessary transitioning of the Church. Revival is going to require major surgery of our expectations and experience of church. Actually we believe the Church is still in its early stages of reformation, but major help is coming now from many quarters. The biblical narratives that were so helpful at this time were and are those again of where God's people have formerly experienced transition. Different ways of relating to each other were required of God's people in the tribal period of the wilderness from when they crossed over to possess the nation. The visitations to the prophets of the exile (Ezekiel, Zechariah, Daniel) prepared them to prepare the people for returning to the land. They had to learn new skills for a new context.

So there was a then and there is a now! It now seemed likely that the fullness of God's purpose for the Charismatic renewal of the Church (1960s–80s) was to get us ready for something as huge as the transformation of society! The thrusting growth and renewal of worship was not an end in itself. As the tribes in the wilderness discovered an identity and a togetherness that was necessary to reform their minds and energise their progress on their coming out of a slavery mentality, so we had discovered and enjoyed a sense of belonging and freedom together in God's presence. But they and we were actually on the way to somewhere else! The identity and freedom were established for a purpose. And that is to possess and dwell in land, where God can dwell also, in and through His people.

And so at this moment of opportunity, the rising experience and excitement of a *'kairos* moment' brings us straight back to this same question, and it is the question of all time. In what sense can the people of God dwell and establish God's Kingdom in a 'secular' environment? How does God's presence affect and indeed reign in a nation rather than just in the Church, and how do God's people exercise that reign? Suddenly our corporate history of Church–State interaction triggers alarm bells, or evokes all sorts of base desires! We discover that we are up against all the mistakes and damage of other seasons of revival at the interaction of God's Kingdom into a fallen world. We are encountering again some unreformed paradigms and expectations. They all relate, as we have said, to our understanding of the Church, the Kingdom and the nature of spiritual authority. If indeed a secular or imperial view and practice of authority has invaded the Church, how can spiritual authority now be exercised out from the Church into the world? These are questions which we must face, and where we get any light, we must obey in order for God to do a fully redemptive thing in and through Europe! Further consideration about the Church and society will obviously follow then, when we have finally finished this review of the issues that God was bringing to our attention, not just cerebrally but through a growing sense of His presence and grace, in preparation for such a major reformation!

## Prepared to Overcome

Of the five waves that we believed the Lord was washing over His people, the fifth was perseverance. Towards the end of the decade, when the revival we had come to expect (in the shape we expected it!) had not occurred, many became disillusioned. This too had a purpose. If the season and therefore shape of the Church is undergoing change, we suggest that it is undergoing the repositioning of the Church into the world. In other terms, it is the transition from a pastor/teacher-shaped Church into a prophetic/apostolic shape. But for this gifting, the apostolic gifting, the qualification is perseverance! It issues in signs and wonders, but Paul does not quote the miracles as his qualification for apostleship but the fact that he has been beat up, pressed down, thrown out and shut in but he is still pressing through! And in this process of an extended transition, we are being tested to the depths of our characters, in order to be ready to carry the necessary power. In fact, there is in process the development and calling out of an overcoming people. They are referred to in many ways in the Scriptures, most notably in Revelation 12, where the Church is seen as a mother giving birth to a man child who has great authority over the enemy who seeks to destroy him. We believe there are moments in church history when the coming forth of such an overcoming people is wonderfully potentially possible, given the coming together of several factors. We believe that today, in Europe, is potentially such a time. One of the key historical biblical factors in the arriving of such a *kairos* moment is a successful generational overlap. The significance of God calling Himself the God of Abraham, Isaac and Jacob is that it takes three overlapping generations to move from a new pioneering beginning in the progress of the Kingdom of God to a point of potential consummation. We see the process repeated as Moses emerges to lead the people out of old captivity and loss into a new context. He trains Joshua and passes on the baton to him and the major struggle then ensues to find a generation that will complete the work that Moses began and Joshua consolidated. Again, Elijah has Elisha following him and developing his pioneering work into its second phase. He, Elisha, does twice as many miracles as his mentor and he functions among a group, a school of prophets, taking the initiative of one breakthrough person into a corporate experience, but even then there is a similar struggle for the third and great advance. It seems there was so much available to pass on! If Joash, the King of Israel, had been able to persevere and press through in banging the arrows of intercession on the ground a few more times, the breakthrough against God's enemies would have been total (2 Kings 13:18f.). But he failed at that hurdle. There was so much grace left over that it stayed in Elisha's bones and was still available to raise a dead man whose body landed capriciously on them (2 Kings 13:21)! This moment of transition between the generations, between seasons, is absolutely pivotal! It connotes a moment of intercessory struggle as in the book of Revelation when even Heaven seems to hold its breath and there *'is silence ... for about half an hour'* (8:1) while we wait to see if the final generation will rise to the challenge. Such glory and breakthrough if they do! And such loss if they don't!

Just as the Scriptures indicate that God visits the sins of the fathers on the children to the third and fourth generation of those that hate Him, but millennial blessings on those that love Him and keep His commandments, the last hundred years in Europe have seen these two streams of blessings and curses running in parallel. At the beginning of the century it looked like the darkness had won. Yet God did not give up and during the century we have seen three generations rise to the promise and restoration of God's blessing. In the early years of the century God heard the prayers and longings of His saints and poured out His presence in the great Pentecostal movement, His compassion and justice in the

Anglo/Catholic stream and His truth in an Evangelical awakening. And His revelation in our nations began to be restored. In the middle years, He moved again and renewal came to both the established and new Churches and His people began to build on His revelation and consolidate and grow in their faith and individual obedience. Now in these last years, He has moved again and increased our longing and our vision of how much more He can and will do concerning the land, the nations, our inheritance, should we be ready for the challenge. Once again we're poised at a window of opportunity which could see the continent swept with either the glory of God or another dark ages. This is what 'calls for the perseverance of the saints' and challenges us to the roots of our being.

## The Returning Children

As the process and themes built up, there was a further sign of extraordinary significance to which we have already referred, to help press us through at a time of great stress. It is the sign of the returning children, a rising tide of men and women, children of empire and mission, coming to these shores. They come with the vision and word for us that the gospel was good seed and they are the fruit of it. They are calling us up into more hope and faith, even new strategies for revival. Biblically, one of the key signs that the exile is over and that the captivity is about to be ended is that of the returning children. In Isaiah 49 when the people of God have no experience but brokenness and barrenness, the Lord's promise is that the *'waste and desolate places and your destroyed land'* will be restored and *'the children of whom you were bereaved'* will come and we will ask *'who has begotten these for me'*, since we are barren (vv. 19, 20, 21). Speaking then of Israel, but down the ages to those of us born of them, the Gentile nations to whom their journeys are an example and a pattern, we have known the blessing and promise of God revealed fully in Jesus Christ, but have fallen back into loss and bereavement. But the sign is the same. He is drawing back the sons and daughters of the gospel to signify a new day of hope and restoration. They come with faith and insight when we are at a loss. Therefore it invokes mercy and humility. We will look in the next chapters at some of the key issues they themselves are bringing to us. But one of the most significant is that their coming forces us to address our reluctance in leadership. We believe there are two aspects to this, and the second, the structural issue, we will address in the following chapter. But here we raise the personal, emotional issues for us in Europe. The result of the choice to sacrifice the sons of Europe has led to a desperate lack of confidence in the sons of the twentieth century to trust fathers, for three generations, leading to a very vulnerable moment. The hearts of the fathers were away from the children and now the hearts of the children are away from fatherhood. We have a deep-seated, inherent but often subconscious reluctance to become fathers or to take on the father role in many of the European nations, especially in England and Germany. We have often blamed lack of mentoring, or lack of fathering for our own immaturity, even though the previous generation has also been suffering from the same lack. Our inability to function as fathers has left us with a crisis in leadership throughout the century which has been addressed by extreme reactions. It has often issued either in extreme lawlessness or weak permissiveness where democracy has had to rule even in church, allowing no strong clear vision to emerge. Or it has manifest in reactionary control where all thought and vision has to be submitted to levels of 'accountability' which stifles and stultifies the body. There is such a great need for healing and forgiveness in this area! Thank God for the major contribution to this coming from those who are our children in the gospel. They can help us. You see, we don't really learn fatherhood from being trained by fathers, although we thank God for many who have been faithful in that role. Their example and patterning will be important. But it is when the child is laid in our arms, when it wriggles and cries and looks into our eyes gazing and searching for recognition, that everything in us cries out, *'Today I have **become** your father'* (Psalm 2:7 NIV). We become fathers as we recognise our children. Thank God for them. They are coming back to us, and we need to listen to them!

## Chapter 4

## Good Seed But Burnt Ground

One of the classic statements of the returning sons of European mission is Ed Silvoso's, when he says,

> We haven't come to tell you anything new. Only to thank you and tell you that the seed that you brought to our land was good, and to remind you what your fathers taught us.

Having said that, and while he honours his Roman Catholic heritage, he unequivocally challenges the syncretistic and state-dominated form that the Roman Catholic Church had taken in the Argentina of the 1950s in which he grew up. It was an expression of Church that denied access to the Scriptures to ordinary people, used state power to prevent non-Catholics from holding public office and left him completely ignorant of personal salvation until his teens. In this context, the good seed he speaks of our fathers bringing is that which brought him to new birth and established him together in living relationship with the worldwide body of Christ. So while we are asserting that living Christianity does survive in those expressions of Church which became invaded with alien spirits of empire during European history, we need to grasp the nettle and attempt some definitions. We need a definition of what the gospel is. Then we need to understand what really constitutes Church, because Church is the agent of the gospel. Finally, we need also to identify the basic biblical means by which the Church carries or expresses the gospel into society. Such definition is not easy in a context where intellectual expressions of the gospel have been and sometimes still are deliberately used to divide the Church and persecute the different parts, where they have been made into weapons of power to reinforce the State or attack true believers. Nevertheless it has to be attempted. So before we go any further we propose to take a few moments to explain our position.

It is our conviction that many of the confusions and theological divisions that happen among biblical Christians are to do with our failure to recognise or understand each other's tools for biblical exegesis. The word 'exegesis' simply means the way we interpret the Scripture. For example, many Bible teachers accept a systematic system of biblical doctrine as a framework for interpreting Scripture. This means that they have already decided the main things that the Bible teaches and so are very unlikely to interpret the Bible in a way that contradicts or alters their received doctrines. There is help for us in this kind of balanced systematic theology which is the result of painstaking work and godly and wise scholarship. But it still has the weakness of being dependent on the revelation and skill of the biblical scholars who decided what was or wasn't important. We always have the problem of human fallibility which we bring to the text. This is why in the end we favour what is referred to as the incarnational or gospel-centred approach. This approach recognises that we accept the authority of Scripture because we first accepted the authority of the Christ of the Scripture. We became Christians because we came to believe that the Jesus of the gospels was both the Jesus of history and the God of eternity. He gave His authority to the Old Testament Scripture which He claimed to fulfil, not abolish (cf. Matthew 5:17–20). He then promised that the Holy Spirit would bring to the memories of the apostles all that He said to them, in so doing giving His authority to the New Testament writings (cf. John 14:26). This approach is based on our attested faith in the Christ of the gospels, and so the gospels become our primary tool for exegesis. Some people call this gospel primacy, not because the gospels are regarded as more truly scripture than the rest of the Bible, but because they are the lens through which we view the rest. For us, what the Lord did and taught in the gospels is the starting point for everything. So we return now to our attempt at basic definitions of gospel and Church.

We will make a start at the heart level, because this is the level at which our returning spiritual children aim. Ed's remarks still make me weep, despite the many times I've heard them. The same is true of the similar statements of my Brazilian and Ugandan friends. Victor Lorenzo from Argentina sums up the problem very succinctly when he says that our hearts are divided from our heads by what has happened in our history in Europe. If, as we suggested in the previous chapter, God Himself is also interested in speaking to us heart to heart we should attempt to listen this way!

## The Seed of the Church

So let's begin with the Lord's heart definition of a living Christian, when discussing who His disciples are with the Father in John 17:3,

> '*And this is eternal life, that they may know You, the only true God, and Jesus Christ whom You have sent.*'     (NKJV)

That this is to do with revelation is clear from His following words, '*I have manifested Your name to the men whom You have given me out of the world*'. It is this personal revelation, new birth or experience of faith that is always the starting point for Jesus. It is this that is in turn the foundation for Church. In my book *Radical Church Planting* (written together with Roger Ellis, Crossways, 1992) I (Roger) explore the definition of Church present in Jesus' first use of the term in Matthew 16:17–19. When the Lord responds to Peter's

statement, '*You are the Christ, the Son of the living God*', it is
with the words,

> '...*flesh and blood did not reveal this to you, but My Father
> who is in heaven. And I also say to you that you are Peter,
> and upon this rock I will build My church.*'

Whatever subsequent controversies may have surrounded
Peter's later role, these verses are clear in indicating that the
Church is built on the rock of revelation. We can say that
the Church is built out of the living stones of people to
whom the Father has given a revelation of who Jesus Christ
is. As Peter himself describes years later,

> '*And coming to Him as a living stone, rejected by men, but
> choice and precious in the sight of God, you also, as living
> stones, are being built up as a spiritual house...*'
>
> (1 Peter 2:4–5)

In the rest of Jesus' words to Peter as recorded by Matthew
we can conclude three further essential characteristics of
church. It is made up of people in the process of discipleship,
as He indicates Peter's growth to maturity; '*blessed are you
Simon, son of John ... I also say to you that you are Peter*'
(Matthew 16:17–18). It is positioned for battle against the
powers of darkness as He indicates when He declares '*the gates
of hell shall not overpower it*' (Matthew 16:18). Finally it is the
agent of the Kingdom of God on earth, as He states:

> '*I will give you the keys of the kingdom of heaven; and
> whatever you shall bind on earth shall be bound in heaven,
> and whatever you shall loose on earth shall be loosed in
> heaven.*'                                       (Matthew 16:19)

These statements of Jesus on the nature of what it is to be
Church make very clear that Church is essentially a generic
reality, something that we are, rather than an institution to
which we belong. This is very important to recognise from

the point of the later confusion of church and state author-ity, where the State did not want people part of it that operated under a different authority alongside theirs. The state authority needed the Church to be the legitimating power, not an alternative one. The issue becomes even clearer when we examine the main definitions of the gospel on the lips of Jesus in the New Testament narratives.

## The Gospel of the Kingdom

Simply put, Jesus speaks of the gospel synonymously in terms of salvation, eternal life and the Kingdom of God, but His use of the term 'Kingdom of God' far and away overshadows the other two terms, and must determine our understanding of them. Roger explores this at length in his book *The Kingdom Factor* (Marshalls, 1985). The heart of the gospel that the Church exists to carry is that Jesus came to announce and usher in the Kingdom of God. He was declar-ing a new way of relating to God, to each other and to planet Earth with its existing kingdoms. He was claiming to be the demonstration of this reality and to be about to secure it forever through His death and resurrection. This of course is what He did. After His resurrection He spent forty days speaking to the apostles about this Kingdom and it is safe to conclude that this was the substance of their gospel too. While the Acts of the Apostles describes the impact of the Kingdom more than it uses the terminology, when it does use the word it is at key points. As we have already seen, Jesus' teaching of the Kingdom begins the book, it is the good news of the Kingdom that Philip preaches in Samaria, and when Paul appoints elders in the first Gentile churches he encourages and strengthens them with the teaching of the Kingdom (14:22–23). Finally we leave Paul in Europe teach-ing the good news of the Kingdom of God in Rome for a full two years.

To summarise then, the gospel is the good news of the Kingdom of God, involving a whole new way of relating to God, one another and the world, encountered by revelation on the basis of repentance and faith. It was initiated and demonstrated by the incarnation of Jesus and secured and established by His death and resurrection. To receive it is to be immediately part of His Church, which exists as a witness to the revelation, a school of discipleship, a spiritual army against the devil and Christ's agent to unlock the Kingdom of God on earth. Writing in the book of Acts, Luke describes the essentials of how the early Church worked this out:

> *'And they were continually devoting themselves to the apostles' teaching and to fellowship, to the breaking of bread and to prayer.'*                          (Acts 2:42)

While this simple lifestyle leads on immediately to more developed expressions of church life and testimony, we would like to suggest that these ingredients of church life were and are the key to having favour with the people and daily church growth. They are the essential means whereby the fire of the gospel of the Kingdom spreads. When these expressions of gospel Christianity have been flourishing in Europe, the Kingdom of God has been strong. Where they have been extinguished or weakened, so has the Kingdom of God.

When John Mulinde describes Europe as burnt ground he is really referring to waves of biblical, Holy Spirit Christianity like this spreading across Europe, yet being extinguished again and again in our history. Burnt ground describes the difficulty of recovery. Wherever fire has passed over ground, it consumes everything that would provide fuel for any other fire. Indeed, land is often burnt deliberately to cause a firebreak, expressly to extinguish other flames. Where fire has been but is now extinguished, the land will not easily sustain another burning. Yet we believe in corporate grace. It is these earlier fires that represent our heritage and spiritual inheritance. It is our conviction that no living word prophesied, no life laid down whether in living or dying and no prayer prayed are ever lost, rather they are ours to be regained. But the difficulty of recovery must not be under-estimated. The spiritual powers of darkness that have repeatedly overcome the light have become strong in so doing. In the last chapter we will investigate them in greater detail as we look at the seven devastated gateway cities and churches of Turkey and understand them in the light of the letters to them in Revelation. But for now we will look at a selection of those outbreaks of gospel fire that burnt across Europe in earlier centuries, those glorious times when the Church really did devote itself to the apostles' teaching, fellowship, the breaking of bread and prayer, and see what we can rediscover of the inheritance yet to be regained.

## Apostles' Teaching

From earliest times following the spread of the work of Paul and Barnabas on the eastern borders of Europe and Asia, the regions around Armenia were wide open to the gospel. It took hold with such success that Armenia was almost certainly the first nation to declare itself a Christian state a century before the conversion of the emperor Constantine. Such was the strength of the move of God there, however, that the exchange of secular for spiritual authority was strongly resisted and a stream of biblical Christianity took root which provided a seed-bed for revival streams for centuries to come. Leaders of apostolic quality rose up among them over the years that devoted their lives to visiting the churches and teaching the Scriptures.

One such was Constantine who changed his name to Silvanus. He first encountered the Scriptures in 653 from a travelling preacher who left behind a manuscript of the four gospels and Paul's epistles as a gift. The study of them changed his life. He made Kibossa in Armenia his base and from there as a centre he worked for the next thirty years teaching and leading many people to Christ. He was so successful that his activities drew the attention of the emperor who issued a decree against the congregations that had come into being and sent one of his officers, Simeon, to execute Silvanus and persecute his followers. In order to humiliate them as much as possible, Simeon and his men gave stones to Silvanus' closest associates and commanded them to stone him to death. They all dropped the stones except one young man whom he had adopted and shown special kindness to. He betrayed and murdered him and was likened to David killing Goliath by the authorities. For all this, Simeon was profoundly moved by all he saw at Kibossa and, like Paul at Stephen's martyrdom, was convicted by the Lord. Three years later he returned to Kibossa and, changing his name to Titus, took up the work and leadership of the man that he had put to death. Later he was also martyred, but the work they left behind continued from strength to strength.

Leo the Isaurian, who became emperor of the eastern or Byzantine empire of Rome early in the century, grew up among these revival Christians and was totally opposed to idolatry either in the worship of icons and images or the growing tendency to venerate the virgin and child. He initiated a movement against idolatry that lasted for three generations and impacted the west of the Roman Empire as well as the east. In 794 the emperor Charlemagne called and presided over the Council of Frankfurt. They set aside the decrees of the second Council of Nicea that had approved the service and adoration of images. (Sadly they did nothing about the anti-Jewish sentiments of that Council.) Nevertheless there was to be no adoration, worship, reverence, or veneration of images; no kneeling, burning of lights or offering of incense and no kissing them, even though representing the virgin and child. They also corrected the teaching that God could only be worshipped in Latin, Greek or Hebrew and insisted that prayer could be made in any language. Charlemagne's heir, Louis, succeeded his father in 813. He was an admirer of a Spanish teacher of the Scriptures called Claudius who was renowned for his Bible commentaries. Louis appointed him Bishop of Turin where he taught publicly that true apostolic ministry was dependent on apostolic life and not on the appointment of man, not even if he were the Bishop of Rome. The impact of these revival streams was massive throughout Europe long before the Reformation, impacting state Christianity like this but never really reforming it because of the State's dependency on it to uphold and not to challenge its authority.

Devotion to the apostles' teaching through the recovery and teaching of the Scriptures was again and again the source of revival. Men like Wycliffe in England, who translated the Scriptures into contemporary English in the fourteenth century, had an enormous impact. It was said that by the end of that century two men could not be found together and one not be a Wycliffite, and that more common people knew the Scriptures than the official clergy did. When summoned to appear before the Pope he declined with the message for him that

> 'Christ during his life on earth was of all men the poorest, casting from him all worldly authority. I deduce from these premises, as a simple counsel of my own, that the Pope should surrender all temporal authority to the civil power and advise his clergy to do the same.'

Wycliffe's teaching powerfully affected Jan Hus, a theological doctor and preacher in Prague. Writing and teaching in the Czech language, his teachings greatly impacted the Slavic people throughout Bohemia, with the result that the Archbishop of Prague excommunicated him and had Wycliffe's writings publicly burned. Subsequently Hus was summoned to the Council of Constance where, despite the emperor's guarantee of safe conduct, he was tried and burnt at the stake for heresy in 1415. Many of Hus's followers understandably but tragically took up arms and there followed thirty years of war that devastated the region. Nevertheless significant revival continued among many of Hus's followers like Peter Cheltschizki who wrote the book *The Net of Faith* in 1440. His words are prophetic for us today:

> 'We are like people who have come to a house that has been burnt down and try to find the original

foundations. This is the more difficult in that the ruins are grown over with all sorts of growths, and many think that these growths are the foundations, and say, "This is the foundation" and "This is the way in which all must go," and others repeat it after them. So that in the novelties that have grown up they think to have found the foundation, whereas they have found something quite different from, and contrary to, the true foundations. This makes the search more difficult, for if all said, "the old foundation has been lost among the ruins", then many would begin to dig and search for it and really to begin a true work of building upon it, as Nehemiah and Zerubbabel did after the destruction of the temple. It is much more difficult now to restore the spiritual ruins, so long fallen down, and get back to the former state, for which no other foundation can be laid than Jesus Christ, from whom the many have wandered away and turned to other gods and made foundations of them.'

## Fellowship

Alongside the many periods of recovering the apostles' doctrine from the Scriptures were glorious periods of discovering and establishing fellowship together in the Holy Spirit. Groups came together and found or re-found one another throughout the course of European church history. Meeting together in small bands for mutual fellowship and encouragement was the way to growth as well as an inevitable threat to the established Church. Some were self-consciously churches, as with the loosely but definitely connected groups of biblical Christians known as Bogomils, Waldenses, and Albigenses throughout the centuries prior to the Reformation. Others formed into monastic communities within the Roman Catholic Church like the Benedictines and Franciscans, or later the Methodist societies that remained throughout John Wesley's lifetime uneasily within the Anglican Church. In the twelfth and thirteenth centuries groups like these existed in large numbers throughout Spain, France, Italy, Germany, Austria and Switzerland. There is great need for intercessors and spiritual mappers to dig into the historical detail of this heritage and unblock these wells of European spiritual life. Their persecution by, and absorption into the State Church of their day tends to cover up some of the most glorious details of the revival flames that burnt in and through them but much of it is there for us to rediscover as we pray and follow revelation by research. The Protestant state Churches for example, that the reformer Zwingli helped institute in the canton of Zurich and those in the adjacent cantons of Bern and St Gallen, were threatened by Christians fellowshipping outside their authority. Between 1523 and 1530 thousands of these Christians were murdered by the authorities with the support and encouragement of the new Protestant state Churches from Zurich to the Tyrol and Salzburg. E.H. Broadbent, a major source of information about these revival moves, writes:

'The spread of the churches in Austria and the surrounding states was marvellous: the accounts of the numbers put to death and of their sufferings are terrible. Of some it is recorded "they went full of joy to their death. While some were being drowned and put to death, the others who were waiting their turn, sang and waited with joy the death which was theirs when the executioner took them in hand. They were firm in the truth which they knew and fortified in the faith which they had from God." Such steadfastness constantly aroused astonishment, and enquiry as to the source of their strength. Many were won by it to the faith, but by the religious leaders, both of the Roman Catholic and reformed churches, it was generally attributed to Satan. The believers themselves said of their colleagues: "They have drunk of the water that flows from the Sanctuary of God, from the well of life, and from this they have obtained a heart that cannot be comprehended by human mind or understanding. They have found that

God helped them to bear the cross and they have overcome the bitterness of death. The fire of God burned in them."'                                    (*op. cit.*)

This is the indestructible seed of the body of Christ that has fallen into the soil of our continent. The new forms and shapes of Church in cell and congregation that are yet to emerge from the burnt ground of Europe will come from the germination of this seed.

## Breaking of Bread

The simple matter of devotion to 'the breaking of bread' was one of the common recurring factors in the revival moves while at the same time it became one of the issues of the greatest contention between them and the state Churches. The theological definitions of transubstantiation versus memorial sign assumed major significance. The Roman Catholic position that the bread and wine became the actual body and blood of Christ during the mass, seen in terms of a re-enactment of the sacrifice of Calvary, leant itself to the need for an officially recognised priesthood to mediate it, which they claimed to represent. This in turn strengthened their position with the state authorities to which they gave legitimacy. The idea that breaking bread was something that ordinary Christians did pretty much whenever they met was extremely undermining of this! The Protestant state Churches, while subscribing to the memorial sign position, still tended to use the communion as an official function, often indicating membership of their Church, as distinct from the Roman Catholic or, in later years, Nonconformist Churches. This use of communion to divide believers or indicate specific local church membership has persisted in various forms down to the present day. The truth is that the breaking of bread is more than just a memorial sign, but it is not a literal re-enactment of the sacrifice of Calvary which was certainly a once-for-all event. Rather it reveals and releases the overcoming power of the cross and resurrection into the moment and place of the event, and as such is, along with baptism, one of the most potent prophetic acts or keys for the release of the Kingdom of God into our space and time. This is why the apostle Paul tells the Corinthians,

> *'For as often as you eat this bread and drink the cup, you proclaim the Lord's death until He comes.'*
>
> (1 Corinthians 11:26)

Ed Silvoso rightly says,

> 'When the church in the city drinks of the cup together and shares the same bread, something happens in the heavenly places that undermines Satan's power in the church, and eventually, the city.'
>
> (*That None Should Perish*, Regal, 1994)

Perhaps this was nowhere more in evidence than in sixteenth-century France, where a movement took place that came close to changing the future of French history. Once again we'll let E.H. Broadbent take up the story:

> 'In 1533 some believers in the south of France were strongly impressed with the need of coming together for the reading of Scripture. At that time Margaret, Queen of Navarre, came from Paris to her husband's territories. With her were Le Fevre and Roussel. They used to attend the Catholic Church in Pau and afterwards hold meetings in the castle, where an address was given on the Scriptures, to which many of the country people came. Some of them expressed the desire to partake of the Lord's Supper, in spite of fears as to the danger of doing this. A large hall was found, however, under the terrace of the castle – a meeting place that could be reached without too much attention. Here at the appointed time, a table was brought, with bread and wine, and all took part in the Supper, without any formality, the Queen and those of the humblest station apprehending

their equality in the presence of the Lord. The word was read and applied, a collection was made for the poor, and the people dispersed.'                    (*op. cit.*)

Imagine the impact on the future of French monarchy and people alike had this prophetic act run its course, which it very nearly did! Within twenty-five years a move of biblical, Holy Spirit Christians, by then generally known as the Huguenots, had planted well over 2000 churches throughout France. Despite massive persecution and massacre, the most famous of which took place in Paris on St Bartholomew's Day in 1572, when Henry of Navarre came to the throne in 1594 he provided an environment in which both Roman Catholics and Huguenots could live in peace. This continued until he was assassinated in 1610, and despite persecution the Huguenots were more or less protected until 1685 when Louis XIV ordered all their pastors to leave France within a fortnight and systematically destroyed their meeting places. Thousands left as exiles for Switzerland, Holland, Germany and Britain. Nevertheless a wonderful movement of ecstatic prophets including bands of child prophets sprang up among those who remained, winning many to faith.

## Prayer

As we look across this whole second day of world mission and examine what went wrong with the European Church, we have to conclude that it has to do with the lack of devotion to prayer. Both in its state church forms and in its revival movements, the glaring missing ingredient of foundational Christianity which time and again left the Church courting the state authority or taking up arms against it was prayer. We are not talking here of devotional or meditative prayer, of which there was much both within the state Church and the revival movements, but prolonged, strategic prayer of the kind that characterised the ministry of Jesus and the apostles. Without it, there was a huge lack of true spiritual authority and government for the Kingdom of God, and in this vacuum the secular authority took over. This is what makes the events of 1727 in Herrnhut so momentous and has drawn many to conclude that if there was one single influence that secured the eventual success of the European mission, this was it. Herrnhut was a wooded hill on the estate of Count Zinzendorf in Saxony, not far from the Czech border. Led by Christian David, refugee descendants of the Moravian believers who had been so devastated during the thirty years' war following the persecution of the Hussites, found protection on the young count's estate. Zinzendorf was in his early twenties, David about ten years older. The hill was originally called Hutberg, or the Watch Hill, but they changed its name to Herrnhut, the Lord's Watch. Here they founded a community where after five years of struggle they were visited by an extraordinary move of the Holy Spirit. There were three main strands to the life of these watchmen. The first was total commitment to the fellowship of the Spirit in relational unity and sacrificial living. The second was a commitment to sustained prayer, both as devoted ministry to the Lord and strategic prayer for the lost. This prayer was unbroken for twenty-four hours a day, seven days a week for over one hundred years! Not surprisingly the third strand was a passion and zeal for world mission that thrust members of the community to the uttermost parts of the earth. Many of them sold themselves into slavery out of zeal to reach slaves in South America. In his book, *The Lost Art of Intercession* (Destiny Image, 1997), Jim Goll describes the impact of their devotion to prayer:

'The Moravians' over one hundred year prayer vigil and global missionary exploits marked one of the purest moves of the Spirit in church history, and it radically changed the expression of Christianity in their age. Many leaders today feel that virtually every great missionary endeavour of the eighteenth and nineteenth centuries – regardless of denominational affiliation – was in a very real sense part of the fruit of the Moravians' sacrificial service and prophetic intercessory prayer. Their influence continues to be felt even in our day. The Lord is clearly planning to increase that influence once again.'

Clearly this is exactly what the Lord is doing as the good seed of their mission in 'the uttermost parts of the earth' focuses informed, strategic, intercession into the 40/70 Window at this time.

## A Present Lull

We saw in Chapter 2 that our failure to complete the Reformation in Europe left the old imperial spirits in place both within the Church and the State. We saw too that the new freedoms released the Humanism that in time became an alternative legitimating power base to Christianity. This worked either by invading the Church again from the inside or else setting up a new power base through political parties and movements vying with the state Churches for influence over state governments. The impact of the First World War on Russia provided the social and political conditions for the breakdown of the Church–State axis of power that had held sway for centuries. As we all know, in 1917 the Communist revolution took place there in which Humanism in its socialist form became the legitimating power base for the imperialistic spirit. The aftermath of the Second World War provided the circumstances in which this was consolidated across central and eastern Europe, the so-called Iron Curtain countries of 1945–89. The collapse of Communism probably amounts to the end of Humanism in its socialist form as the legitimating shape for European governments. In its aftermath, the idolatry of national identity and the re-emergence of the old state Churches, particularly the Eastern Orthodox Churches, is growing and vying for influence. Islam, of course, is a potent alternative to Christianity along the ancient borders of eastern Christendom and beginning to be so within the immigrant communities of the inner cities throughout the continent. Nevertheless today the vast majority of Europeans, east and west, look with hope and expectation for the various capitalist, free enterprise forms of Humanism that have developed in western Europe to provide the social legitimation and shape for the future. However, from the biblical perspective of the Kingdom of God we have to face the reality that Humanism itself is the product of an uncompleted reformation that failed to exorcise either Church or society from the demons of imperialism. Far from expecting these forms of Humanism to provide freedom for the gospel or justice for the peoples of Europe all the evidence is to the contrary.

A simple exposition of Old Testament Scripture makes clear that the reason for the judgement of God on the Canaanite people was their commitment to sexual immorality and occult practice as normal social behaviour (Leviticus 18; Deuteronomy 18:9–14). In the light of the incarnation we can say that the only reason for God to exterminate them was that their practices provided evidence of the enthronement of demonic powers. These powers were so opposed to the Kingdom of God that to let the states they inhabited continue to exist would be to have given up hope of the Kingdom of God ever coming. Since the incarnation and triumph of the cross we know that individuals and nations can be separated from their demons and whole cities, nations and indeed continents can and must be saved. But given that the same practices are our norms for social behaviour in contemporary democratic free enterprise Europe, the application of the Scripture suggests that the same demonic powers destructive to the Kingdom of God are enthroned here. If we pursue this theme further in the Old Testament we discover that the root sins behind these practices are the social injustices of which we in the West are the most guilty. The city states of Sodom and Gomorrah were representative of these same immoral and occult practices. The Scripture contains the following revealing analysis:

*'Behold, this was the guilt of your sister Sodom: she and her daughters had arrogance, abundant food, and careless ease,*

> *but she did not help the poor and needy. Thus they were*
> *haughty and committed abominations before Me. Therefore I*
> *removed them when I saw it.'*            (Ezekiel 16:49–50)

This is an accurate assessment of western Europe where free enterprise Humanism is the most strongly established. The point we are making here is that Europe is at this time in a lull between the old state church pressures that resisted biblical, Holy Spirit Christianity and the state Humanism pressures that opposed the gospel in eastern and central Europe under Communism. While we believe that the captivity is over, it will not be over for long. Soon the powers still inhabiting democratic, capitalist Europe will strengthen themselves. Government and society leaders will realise again, as some already do, that the Church of Jesus Christ represents another kingdom to theirs and will set out to oppose it directly once again. God has opened a window of opportunity through the seed of the gospel. He is calling for the Church in the nations of Europe to rise up in their redemptive calling at this time and in partnership with the nations of the third day Church to release an onslaught of strategic prayer that will exorcise our Churches and nations of the imperialistic spirits that are destroying the work of the Kingdom of God. At the same time He is looking to release new expressions of devotion to the apostles' teaching, fellowship, breaking of bread and prayer throughout the streets, cities and regions of the nations of Europe, penetrating and invading all the spheres of European society.

## Redemptive Purpose

In this process the key redemptive purposes of the different European nations come into play. The Church in the eastern and central European nations of the old Communist bloc has a particularly important role at this time. They have lived through and learnt to contend with the pressures from Humanism in its socialist form. They have played their part in breaking the spiritual strongholds that were shaping and controlling their nations. We desperately need to hear their story and receive their input into Europe as a whole. We believe that every one of the forty-eight nations of Europe has a key part to play in the re-evangelising of Europe. Each has, we believe, not only a distinct personality or creation glory, but also a distinctive redemptive purpose, since in whichever way it has been moulded by its history, in both the good and the bad times, it can now release the redemptive wisdom of that experience. We are familiar with the idea in the Scriptures of the way that the cross brings redemption out of the worst situations and events in the lives of individuals. That is the very power and glory of our gospel. The worst thing that could possibly have happened to the most perfect man that ever lived was that He be despised, rejected and, though innocent and good, be convicted and killed. Yet it was this very experience that changed the course of the world since it gave the opportunity of turning the worst evil to the greatest good. The torture and killing of an innocent man is not a good thing! But the power of the gospel is that God is kind enough and His love is powerful enough that in any situation He is able to absorb the evil and overcome it by an opposite spirit! So when Jesus was reviled, He forgave. And the evil strength of those rejecting, hurtful words was not just ignored, it was neutralised, it was disempowered. When He was tortured and hung on the cross, He did not rail against His killers but prayed for them. So the worst situation became a gateway for the most extreme release of love. And this is the power of the gospel also released in and through us who believe. Paul writes that '... *all things work together for good with them that love God and are called according to His purpose*' (Romans 8:28). This is not a fatalistic statement of 'Qué sera sera'! It means that in any and every situation that we find ourselves we are there for a purpose, a redemptive purpose, to encounter every opposition to God's love and glory, to draw it away into the cross and to release the overcoming power of the Kingdom of love instead. As we look for the shape that our experiences, good or bad, have formed in us we see its redemptive moulding – how that effect in us can also be channelled or used for Kingdom purposes. It is to do with the character and disposition formed through adverse experiences. The Genesis story of Joseph is the best narrative of these principles. His creation gift was obviously vision, so he dreamt big dreams and got himself into all sorts of hot water by speaking too soon. Creation gift often has a lot to do with the subsequent responses that happen to us which can then go on to mould us. As a result of provoking his brothers, he was sold into slavery, suffered prison but finally came to the notice and subsequent service of the Pharaoh and ruled his kingdom. He himself said to his brothers that they *'meant evil against me, but God meant it for good in order to bring about this present result, to preserve many people alive'* (Genesis 50:20). Let us say again that what happened to him and what happens to us in so many ways in a fallen world full of fallen people is not good, it is evil. God does not send evil or cause evil things to happen to us because *'he only does wonderful things'* (Psalm 72:18). But the genius of the gospel, the power of Christ's death and resurrection, is that if we will meet any and all circumstances with faith in the power of God's Kingdom, God can work it **for** good and reveal a higher purpose. The redemptive moulding process in Joseph's experience was that he learnt humility and perseverance. In those circumstances, without faith, he **could** have been moulded into bitterness and despair. Redemptive moulding is the character of Christ that is formed in the furnace of testing. The result of evil circumstances causing more of Christ to be formed in the earth is truly redemptive.

Now many of us will have no difficulty with this discourse so far. Yet it may get a little more complicated to talk this way about nations. Do nations have creation gifts? We believe they do and we will look at some biblical suggestions in the next chapter. Do nations have redemptive purpose? Biblically, of course they do, and most people outside Europe who don't suffer from the tendency to think only in individual terms will have no problem with this. But we Europeans, and particularly those of us who have learnt our theology in the English language or from those who learnt theirs that way, are often blind to the application of the cross to corporate entities such as cities or nations. In the story of Joseph cited earlier his personal history clearly became redemptive for both Egypt and Israel. As a result the present and future of both nations was changed forever. The cross of Christ worked for the salvation of individuals precisely because He died for the sins of the world. A nation or a city can fail to lay hold of the atonement, as Jesus prophetically warned Jerusalem. But if the intercessory principle is applied, the whole history of a city, a nation, or even a continent, can be changed. Look at what happened to Jerusalem which was warned that it was missing its day of visitation! From 120 to 3000 in a weekend and the whole city filled with Jesus' teaching within weeks! Such is the power of the cross. If we apply faith in the gospel's redemptive power to our historical circumstances, then when we are functioning as kingly priests for our nation, we can effect change and redemption through our prayers and intervention and this is our prayer and longing for the nations of Europe. Certainly the wisdom of overcoming in one national experience could serve another brother nation, as we suggested as a way in which the European nations of the former Communist bloc could help the westerners. Can nations experience redemptive moulding? Certainly in the history of Israel we see again and again that they are changed and transformed when they learn from their mistakes and when they listen to their prophets. We take great hope from the visionary insight of the Ugandans who were moulded through the dreadful traumas of their national experience into such sweet sensitivity. We believe that the redemptive moulding of the European colonial history may well be a new humility, so help us God.

## The Significance of Nations

While this is obvious to many, it is new vocabulary to some and new theology for others. It is so important at this time that we need to make sure that the biblical revelation is as clear as possible. Some of us have even been beguiled into the error of believing that nations have no ongoing significance in the work of the Kingdom of God. We have falsely concluded that the one new nation, the new humanity of the New Testament epistles, excludes any distinctive contribution for national tribes and their identities. But this is far from the biblical picture. The Jews and the Gentile tribes are not merged by the blood of the cross in Ephesians 2. They are reconciled. Absolutely we are God's household but this does not alter the fact that we are from *'every tribe and tongue and people and nation'* (Revelation 5:9). In the New Jerusalem *'the nations shall walk by its light, and the kings of the earth shall bring their glory into it'* (Revelation 21:24).

Only this view makes sense of the Old Testament. Abraham was promised that he would be the *'father of many nations'* (Genesis 17:4). This promise passed only through Isaac. Some of us have thought mistakenly that it was fulfilled through the other sons of Abraham and their descendants becoming the nations that Abraham fathered. But this cannot be the meaning if it is part of the covenant promise. This is not to devalue the significance before God of those nations outside the Old Testament covenant, but simply to point out that they were not the fulfilment of God's promise to Abraham. This becomes clearest of all when the promise is passed on to Joseph's son by Jacob at the end of his life (cf. Genesis 48:19). It makes it one hundred per cent clear to us that this 'father of nations' promise was not fulfilled in Old Testament days, for by Joseph's time all the non-Jewish descendants of Abraham and Isaac were already established as nations and the promise was still unfulfilled. For the promise to be fulfilled it was necessary for Jesus to come. It is He who is the father of many nations – the father of those nations that proceed from the remnant of the nations of the earth as they turn to Him. This is what the prophets are looking forward to when they speak of a redeemed remnant of the Philistines, of Egypt and so on (cf. Zechariah 9:6–7). This is what the Father is calling forth from the nations of Europe at this time so that the European parts of the one new humanity may come to fullness. The word 'gentile' literally means ethnic tribes or nations apart from the Jews. So we can accurately paraphrase Paul's words to the church in Ephesus, that gateway city for Europe, as follows:

> 'But now in Christ Jesus you who formerly were far off have been brought near by the blood of Christ. For He Himself is our peace, who made the tribes of Europe (as well of the rest of the continents) and the Jews into one, and broke down the barrier of the dividing wall.'
>
> (cf. Ephesians 2:13–14)

It is essential that this reconciliation that Christ has won for us on the cross becomes a present reality in our experience today. This is no easy matter here in Europe where we have nearly two millennia of sin and enmity to deal with. This is true both in terms of the sin of individuals and the corporate sin of Church and nation inhabited by demonic powers of the empires and enemies of the Kingdom of God. But this is why it needed the cross and why we have the cross. All dominion will yet be given to the children of the saints of the Most High God among the peoples and lands of this wonderful continent.

## *Chapter 5*

# The Cry of the Land!

## Roots and Identity

Consideration of the history of the peoples of our continent, particularly in the present context of the many upheavals and conflicts in Europe and the political questions concerning our future relationships has, in recent years, caused a great searching for an understanding of our national identities or continental identity. Often national identities are defined rather by what they are not than their essential nature. The Scottish, Welsh and Irish are definitely 'not English', the Belgians 'not French', as the Canadians are 'not American'. In a continent where the flow of tribes, peoples and languages has waxed and waned over millennia, it has become increasingly difficult to discern our deepest roots, so we often find ourselves clinging to the security of our most recent social or political definition and resisting any other. Yet an interesting new development in the discussion about identity is the resurgence of interest in the Celtic tradition, which peoples seem to have some of the most ancient roots in Europe.

'Many of the names of the Celtic tribes are still familiar today: the Galli of Gaul, the Belgae of north-eastern Gaul and the Galatae of Galatia in Asia Minor ... Celtici survived to Roman times in south-western Spain ... The Greek writer Herodotus mentions the Keltoi in passing in the mid-fifth century BC when writing about the source of the River Danube ... It seems that at this time Celtic people stretched form the Upper Danube region round to northern Portugal. (Then) they migrated south into Italy and the Balkans, west to Iberia, east to Asia Minor and north to the mouth of the Rhine and across to the British Isles.'

(Roger Ellis and Chris Seaton,
*The New Celts*, Kingsway Publications, 1988)

This interest in all things Celtic has surfaced culturally as well as in new expressions of worship and lifestyle in some church streams and as such has caused major questioning. Its influence is clearly seen in the New Age movement, with many shops selling crystals, incense and other occultic artefacts also carrying jewellery ranges marked with Celtic symbols. Does Celtic therefore not equal druidic, animistic and is it not therefore inappropriate to a Christian search for identity and biblical relevance? And even though these tribes mentioned may well have something of a common European identity, they were pre-Christian, darkened and needed the coming of the gospel to civilise and save them.

We thank God that the gospel did indeed reach the Celtic peoples after they had been overwhelmed and pushed to the fringes of the continent by the Roman and Barbarian invasions. Yet as modern missiologists will testify, the coming of the gospel to a people should not overwhelm and subdue their inherent culture and personality, but enlighten and fulfil it. And as the gospel was received in these regions, it took on a different form and expression than that more common in the Roman and Greek worlds. Much has been discussed about the possibility of syncretism, where druidic or animist practices were simply overlaid with Christian doctrine, or, slightly more acceptably, re-interpreted in the light of the incarnation. Of course we must be aware of these possibilities, but this is equally true of all cultures.

'... *Jews ask for signs and Greeks search for wisdom; but we preach Christ crucified, to Jews a stumbling block and to Gentiles foolishness, but to those who are the called, both Jews and Greeks, the power of God and the wisdom of God.'*
(1 Corinthians 1:22–24)

The revelation of Christ must reach into all cultures, and all cultural environments will be challenged and changed by Him. But He will also be revealed in and through them, and it is in the wealth of such revelation coming together from all tribes that we will see His fullness. As Isaiah prophesied, *'the fullness of the whole earth is His glory!'* (Isaiah 6:3, alternative reading).

## Cultural Strengths and Weaknesses

Noel O'Donoghue writes of the cultures which first carried the gospel into the Gentile world, and we affirm with him the different strengths which those nations brought to the propagating of the gospel as well as appreciating his insights into the long-term effects of cultural dominance:

'Greek philosophy and culture was the first ambience or environment into which Christianity came, and our theology is largely an amalgam of Hebrew and Greek ways of presenting the Christ-event and its shattering and transforming implications ... On the other hand, there is the Roman influence in which hierarchy and authority are supreme. This provides a wonderful harmony of order and discipline ... As it has developed over the centuries, this Roman authoritarian approach does not reject the Greek tradition of speculation and scholarship but rather tames and domesticates it, deciding what is to be taught, laying down limits to free speculation, above all choosing safe and sound men as bishops and teachers. When it is tempered with kindness and compassion and a real sense of the Cross of Christ this kind of theology and practice provides a

reasonably happy atmosphere for all except those who
wish to think for themselves in a radical and challenging way.'
(*The Mountain Behind the Mountain*, T&T Clark, 1993)

Now we are certainly not promoting a gospel different in
any way than Jesus Christ revealed in the gospels, preached
by the apostles and taught by the writers of the Scriptures!
What we are saying is that the reception of the gospel will
evoke different responses and be incarnated with different
biases as it comes to peoples and cultures that are themselves
formed by different influences and experiences. The way in
which the Messianic believers responded to the revelation of
Christ was clearly different from that of the early Gentile
believers and it needed some working out, both in the
Scriptures themselves and in subsequent generations of
praxis. But as the same Lord Jesus Christ is born in different
peoples, times and cultures, and as in the mix and interaction of these 'iron sharpens iron', we get a fuller and fuller
revelation of His glory in and through all of creation. The
grace of God in the Roman character and culture prepares
them the more easily to understand the discipline and
authority of Christ as O'Donoghue points out. This is already
illustrated in the gospel itself by the centurion whom the
Lord praised for his faith. He truly understood by revelation
how to exercise the authority of heaven when he saw how
Jesus functioned in relationship to His heavenly Father. The
Lamb slain from the foundation of the earth was the one
who would freely choose to humble Himself and show in His
own obedience as a man the power of the freely laid down
life. So the centurion could relate to this flow of authority: *'I
too am a man under authority with soldiers under me, and I say to
one "Go" and he goes . . . '* (Luke 7:8). The gift of the Greeks in
seeking wisdom and insight, in developing philosophy and
enquiry, is also patterned in the biblical narrative by those
early enquirers who came to Andrew because they would *'see
Jesus'* (John 12:21). Now the particular, as we would say,
creational gifts of these nations are also open to abuse or

subversion, as we have spent quite a few chapters pointing out, in the development of a hierarchical, imperialistic dominating authority that emanated from the fallen use of the Roman grace. When authority is not submitted to the higher, loving serving authority of God Himself, it ends up in the self-seeking 'might is right' bully-boy tactics which crucifies humble loving servanthood! The gift of open-minded enquiry can also become distorted as Paul pointed out in Athens, when the Greek gift becomes so committed to seeking, it cannot close on truth. They even raise an idol to that which they don't yet know, making an idolatry of the pursuit of knowledge. As such they may forever be tempted to remain those who are *'always learning and never able to come to the knowledge of the truth'* (2 Timothy 3:7). The gift of the Celtic peoples may be more easily subverted to animistic spiritism, but may equally be redemptively sensitive to insights of Holy Spirit truth and lifestyle that we could learn from.

## Desert Fathers

So, as the gospel arrived among our ancient Celtic fore-fathers, it was received and understood in a cultural mindset that perceived the revelation of Christ in its own unique way and offered its own particular insights. It was as 'a defeated race the Celts were ready to receive the religion of the cross and the resurrection' (O'Donoghue, *The Mountain Behind the Mountain*) which already distinguishes the Celtic paradigm from that of the vaunting colonists. In fact, it is likely that the stream of revelation of Christ that reached the Celtic peoples did even come via an alternative cultural expression than that which came in the providence of God through the Roman domination of Europe. There is evidence of vibrant trade routes between Alexandria, Constantinople and the British Isles via Gibraltar, and there are many signs in early forms of Celtic Christianity of more eastern traditions in their artwork, and specifically in their dating of Easter. 'It does seem clear that there was a strong influence upon

the early native Christian community in these islands
from the "desert fathers" of Egypt, Palestine and Syria' (Ellis
and Seaton, *The New Celts*). These early missionaries were
Christians who had imbibed an experience of the gospel
that survived persecution and was triumphant in the face
of oppression. As the early Christians were scattered, im-
prisoned, tortured and martyred by decadent Rome, they
rejoiced in God's presence and power. But after the conversion of Constantine, Christianity itself went through a
paradigm shift from a despised, oppressed, suffering community, after the image of the suffering servant Christ, to an
increasingly powerful majority, where state and church
power coalesced. For some this seemed alien to the gospel
they had received and they did not know how to function in
this new Christian order. They retreated therefore to the
deserts, the wilderness places 'outside the camp', and lived
either solitary hermit existences or formed small communities, where the spiritual disciplines associated biblically with
wilderness experience were central to their lifestyles: fasting,
solitude, simplicity and, indeed, forms of self-imposed suffering. Many came out to them to receive wisdom, teaching,
challenge and consolation, and their influence and faithful
witness spread along the North African trade routes, coming
finally to these far-flung shores. Here, their experience
resonated with the Celtic peoples who had also by now been
'hammered into the ground by the Roman legions and the
Barbarian invasions ... As a defeated race the Celts were
ready to receive the religion of the cross and resurrection'
(O'Donaghue, *The Mountain Behind the Mountain*).

So what is the particular intrinsic glory of the Celtic
peoples, the mark of the image of God in them through their
very creation, which the redemptive power of the gospel will
draw up, highlight and enrich, and through which the gospel
itself will be expressed and illumined to others? Bishop
Simon Barrington-Ward writes,

> 'The Celtic world had its own special richness. Its flashes
> of brilliant ornamentation, its wild joy in human pleas-

ure and achievement, in war and gigantic acts of heroism, in lust and passionate love. Its arts and skills and arcane learning were shot through with gleams of the Spirit. But it was haunted again and again by fear and tragedy, presided over by dark powers, threatened with transience and final emptiness. At the very moment of its falling apart, the Celtic saints suddenly emerged to embody a new beauty, attracting those around them by their sheer holiness and wholeness.'

(Foreword to *Restoring the Woven Cord*
by Michael Mitton, DLT, 1995)

Although at first glance it may seem there would be a discord about the gospel of the ascetic desert fathers in their choice to withdraw prophetically from worldly culture appealing to the life-affirming, potentially abandoned Celts, their sensitivity, their imaginative intuition made them very accepting of the life of the unseen world, and their experience of warfare and conflict there would have made the resurrection triumph of Christ very attractive. Perhaps their very wholeheartedness made for a resonance with the gospel lived and shared by those willing to die for its truth. And so for our Celtic forebears,

'the rigid discipline of the desert fathers ... was mixed with a life-affirming worldview. They loved life and celebration, but they did not indulge their bodies ... It was Augustine of Hippo's neoplatonism that taught the rigid separation of the spiritual and the material worlds and which casts such a long shadow across the landscape of western thinking. In contrast, the worldview of the Celts was remarkably holistic.'

(Ellis and Seaton, *The New Celts*)

Many writers will draw on different aspects of Celtic Christian teaching and practice, but it is their love for the land, their spiritual relationship with the whole of creation that is the particular aspect of our present interest and, we

believe, one of the redemptive gifts of nations which we have
need, and perhaps inheritance right, to draw from.

## Holistic Worldview

Now, though we do recognise the grace on all peoples to
discern life and revelation from the Scriptures, in order that
'the wealth of the nations' will come to Him, the fact
that Jesus was born into a particular time and cultural
context must give us some eternal biases! If the Word was
made flesh in the fullness of time, the place and people
among whom He was first revealed must carry a particular
congruence with God's eternal truth. This would seem the
more obviously so, given the time God had invested in
preparing such a people over many generations, with guidance from the Law, the prophets and a great deal of historical
narrative, to bring them to the point where Jesus came forth
among them. And because of this, we do presume that the
Hebrew worldview is essentially a more precise framework for
understanding revelation than others. In this regard, it seems
that our Celtic forefathers were blessed with a closer match
than the subsequent paradigm that we have inherited
today of the neoplatonism to which Chris Seaton refers.
In his cutting-edge book, essential reading for European
Christians struggling with the changing worldview that,
like it or not, we are subject to in this present 'millennial'
moment, Jim Thwaites sums it up this way:

> 'For the Hebrew, the spiritual or unseen realm was one
> with the created realm. It did not exist in a separate or
> removed dimension; it was in union with all of life and
> creation. The spiritual dimension of life is the heart or
> essence of every created thing, both seen and unseen ...
> What we have generally called the "spiritual realm"
> was, to the Hebrew mind, simply the unseen realm. The
> Greeks saw the spiritual realm as disconnected from the
> material and relational world. For them it began in
> the angelic realm and moved away from there into a

transcendent heaven removed from life. The Hebrews would never have tolerated such blurred vision. For them the spiritual encompassed all of life.'

(*The Church Beyond the Congregation*, Paternoster, 1999)

For even as the Trinity considered, dreamed and planned to bring about creation, as Love manifested themselves as ever giving, ever increasing, ever searching for wider, wilder, deeper, richer contexts to reach and serve into, Love was revealed in that which they created. Creation is not just a picture about God: it is His very voice.

> 'His eternal ... nature [is] *clearly seen through what has been made.'* (Romans 1:20)

So, as we meditate on the depths of the creation story, we draw on a new understanding and relationship with our God, and the creation also teaches us.

For three days God formed things. By His Spirit and Word, He conceived, brooded and spoke into being new forms from that which already existed. By speaking, He formed light and dark. His Word called them into visible definition and they were formed and separated because light now was distinct in the darkness and darkness was now revealed by the light. By naming the earthly heavens, the firmament, He drew them out from the waters of the heavens and the earth He also called out from the heavenly waters, 'the dry from the wet'. So the earth that had been 'without form' was now defined and formed. But all that was formed was formed from the deep waters that always existed, the very presence and voice of God Himself.

> 'In the beginning was the Word ... All things came into being by Him, and apart from Him nothing came into being that has come into being.' (John 1:1, 3)

Then for three more days God filled that which had been void or empty. Heaven filled the firmament with vessels of light, and the earth produced vegetation and marvellous creatures, fish and birds. Great sea monsters dived to the depths, myriad creatures fanned out to the East and the West, and the birds, created out of the earth, flew up into the heavens. Like Love Himself, that which was formed from His Word and Presence would reach up, down and out to fill all things with His revelation. And the heavenly images, the lights in the firmament, shone downward, pouring warmth, life and health into the earth by day, and gentle consolation for rest by night. Finally at the peak of creation, Man who was formed of the manifest dust of the earth, was also filled with the unseen breath of heaven. In the heart of the heavenly places there is a core which is now visible. And in that core which is now formed, defined within the unseen realm to be seen, the interdependence of the seen with the unseen is clearly depicted. More than a picture or a parable, the creation is the 'ultimate myth', a true seen expression of an unseen reality. Formed of the word of God, it continues to speak and express that which made it, despite the scrambling or distortion of the message by the subsequent abuse of the vessel – this wholeness of the creation revealing the unseen world the Celts particularly understood, as did the Hebrews. The very earth, the land itself, comes from and links to the heavens of God and man stands at the visible interface. Surely with this in mind, God, who had already created Adam and Eve out of the dust of the land and placed them in a garden as a pattern of how to relate to and subdue the land beyond those boundaries, also called a new family to leave one piece of land to go and inhabit another, so that God Himself, in and with them, could live there with them! And how significant it is that when the Scriptures introduce Jesus as coming from the unseen world into our visible one, they relate His coming to how His forefathers were related to the land.

> *'Therefore all the generations from Abraham to David are fourteen generations; and from David to the deportation to Babylon fourteen generations; and from the deportation to Babylon to the time of Christ fourteen generations.'*
>
> (Matthew 1:17)

## The Created Order Begins With Land

We are aware that the created order relates to much more than land simply. The establishment of communities, cities, civilisation and all the attending stuff of human life and spheres of activity are facets of human creativity stemming from and reflecting back into the creation of God Himself. All of it, as the Celts realised, is the proper arena for carrying and speaking the glory of God, and this we will also consider further later. Yet the reaching and subduing of territory precedes dwelling in it. A geographical, territorial aspect to the gospel has often been overlooked by our systematic theologies. When reading of the land, we often simply understood the specific land of Israel as in view as a background context for some greater story being told upon it. But if God named a land from a people and led them to dwell in such a land, it would be for a specific purpose and, as ever with His chosen people, that purpose would be for a sign to all other nations to learn from and follow. The battles for that particular tiny strip of land in the Middle East that have ensued over generations even up to the present day, should signal a strong marker for us of the significance of land itself.

## Land and Identity

From this perspective, as European peoples we cannot divorce our search for identity, understand our history and relationships, our calling and destiny in God, nor our perception of how He means now to move and act again, from our understanding of the land we are created from and called to. John Dawson, a man whom God has used across the world in the ministry of reconciliation between people groups, genders and generations, has made some remarkable observations about the nature of land and in particular the 'first nation's people' who live there. It is as if those who are the most closely and long term related to a particular land still resonate with that creation. Adam was made from the earth, but then he was given the breath of God. Now God is

Word, and so with His breath comes the power of speech. So Adam becomes able to articulate what the dust of creation is speaking. John Dawson tells the story of being in New Zealand and Australia. Now these are two nations reasonably recently inhabited by European peoples who have become the dominant people groups there. Both national groups come from very similar stock. Originally British, they left, many against their will, as criminally deported (we use the juxtaposition of words advisedly!) or displaced by land clearances. Some were adventurers, explorers; others were seeking a better life for their families. They came to the land: some in the rolling hills and steaming geysers of the smaller islands of New Zealand, the others in the vast expanses, the hot desert rocks, the endless bush and the glorious coasts of vast Australia. Some hundred or so years later, the armies of these two nations, originally from the same ethnically European stock, join together in the Anzac forces to fight in the war. Though one force, they are immediately noted for their different strengths and weaknesses. The New Zealanders are fearless, immediately bold, the Australians persevering, consistent. John Dawson makes a striking parallel with the different first nation's peoples of the respective lands. The Maori have lived in the New Zealand islands for generations. The world knows them now for the Haaka, the tribal war dance used by the New Zealand rugby team before their matches. Anyone watching knows the aggression is real and no token ceremony! The Maori are assertive, wild, immediate, not dissimilar to the springs gushing somewhat unpredictably but with untold force and power from the depths of the earth in Rotorua. The landmass of New Zealand is narrow, broken up. One can't walk many days before having to stop. By contrast, the Australian Aboriginals are slow talking, slow moving but long term as befits a people with vast, seemingly unlimited terrain to travel through in extremes of oppressive heat. They hold themselves in, pacing themselves for the long haul. A sudden, warlike, breakthrough gift and a persevering, long-term, faithful grace, both reflecting the shape of the land, manifested and expressed through the cultural glories of first nation's people, but which also seemed to be absorbed and imbibed by those arriving later to dwell in the same land.

Our point is this: we have a creation-given link with land and a redemption mandate that takes us back to the land. We do not want to be misunderstood in any way to be saying that certain people need to live in certain places and the horrendous corollary of that position that disempowers and dishonours all people who, over generations and for very many reasons, have moved from one land to another. As we have said, God has a particular and marvellous role and purpose for such peoples. Indeed, Christ Himself says,

> *'Truly ... there is no-one who has left houses or brothers or sisters or mother or father or children or farms for My sake and for the gospel's sake, but that he shall receive a hundred times as much now in this present age ... with persecutions...'*
> (Mark 10:29–30)

In many cases, peoples have been moved and dispossessed. Their leaving their lands was not consciously for the sake of the Lord. But in the plans and purposes of God, their new location can be embraced as for His sake, and the persecutions already suffered can become the redemptive process that helps gain His Kingdom. Many of us European peoples may not know exactly which area of this great continent we originated from. But all the land is groaning for a voice and Christians are being recalled to *'dwell in the land'*.

> *'The righteous will inherit the land,*
> *And dwell in it forever.'*
> (Psalm 37:29)

The paradigm that separates spirituality from the created order leaves us the poorer. Not only do we suffer from a rootlessness and dislocation, but also from loss of identity and indeed authority as our creation mandate was to be in right, authoritative relationship with the earth from which we were made. But the land too suffers, and God calls a people throughout His Word, not just to dwell in the land so they may be blessed, fed and comfortable, but that the land itself should be healed. Our origins may give us some insights to the redemptive gift of the nation that we are ethnically related to and that may be helpful to better understand our gifts and callings. We should be encouraged to draw on the wealth of our generational and geographical corporate history. It is an inheritance of which we have need in these days and to which we have a God-given right. But our present location also is an inheritance and a calling. Wherever we find ourselves positioned today, it is for the blessing of the land and it is urgent that we embrace the calling to connect with the fullness of the creation, to express its voice, its groaning to the heavens and to receive back from God the flow of His life, presence and Word to reach to the depths and width of all that He called into being to reveal His glory.

## Our Priestly Role

Michael Mitton quotes Noel O'Donaghue talking about 'the priestly role of the church in bringing together the divine and human worlds'. Mitton goes on,

> 'We have been entrusted with the work of blessing our land; but if we fail to do this, there are principalities and powers of darkness that are all too ready to contaminate the earth. Our failure to take this priestly duty seriously has allowed much darkness to spread in our lands.'
>
> (*Restoring the Woven Cord*)

The Scripture highlights this priestly role on behalf of the land in these very famous verses, calling us to repentance:

> *'If I shut up the heavens so that there is no rain, or ... if I send pestilence ... and My people who are called by My name humble themselves and pray, and seek My face and turn from their wicked ways, then I will hear from heaven, forgive their sin and will heal their land.'* (2 Chronicles 7:13–14)

It shows that sin, dislocation from God and from living according to His plans and purposes in all our ways, has a direct effect on the land. The land itself witnesses to unright-eousness, or the not-rightness of how things are. Part of the dynamic of God speaking prophetically to bring men and women back to walking rightly is by *'wonders in the heavens and in the earth'* (Joel 2:30 NKJV). Again and again in the Scriptures the Lord speaks to His people of repentance, change, hope and deliverance through the state of the created order. Only twenty-first-century Europeans choose not to listen to this language, even though, for instance, the extraordinary attention-demanding hurricanes in Britain were repeated at the turn of the millennial year in France. Even though floods of truly unusual intensity have risen across the continent. Even though the weather patterns are changing inexorably, coinciding with remarkable phenom-ena in the sky: Halley's comet, intense 'shooting star activity' and the full total eclipse of the sun, clearly visible on a trajectory across much of our continent. Yes, it may be explainable in terms of global warming and ozone layers, but the question should not only be 'how' are these things happening, but 'why'. The whole of creation is groaning, and it needs a response and a voice from those who know and love God and are called according to His purpose in and through all of creation.

## Reconciling All Things

God's intention in Christ is to *'reconcile all things'* (Colossians 1:20). What needs reconciling? Many areas of breakdown are clearly obvious to us from our own experience of pain. We are out of sorts with one another and our relationships need reconciling. Men and women misunderstand each other, generations clash in worldview and culture, nation wars against nation. Even a cursory reading of the early chapters of Genesis will map out where the areas of breakdown began for us. Adam and Eve blame and shame each other. The gifts and callings that they represent, the intuitive, imaginative

gift and the logical, rational process disrespect each other.
Cain is jealous of his brother. The skills and dispositions
that Cain and Abel represent, compete and kill rather than
complete and honour each other. The flood baptises the lot
and God gives Noah's family a fresh start, but the elder
provokes the younger and the son despises the father. By the
tower of Babel, they all have to be separated. The languages
are confused; people groups form and begin to wander over
the face of the land.

But what is the significance of Babel, and why do they end
up wandering? It's because the first place of rupture that took
place in the beautiful wholeness of Eden was between the
glory of God's heavenly presence and humankind. As God
came through from the unseen realm into the defined realm
in the cool of the day, Adam and Eve withdrew so as not to be
seen. He who was hidden but who chose to become manifest
for their sakes, was rejected as Adam and Eve chose to hide
themselves from Him because of their shame. They caused a
barrier or rift to be formed between the manifest presence of
God and their own. The immediate result of that rift was a
corresponding dislocation between the man and the earth,
which reflected the presence of God. Like a mirror image of
the heavens, as man rejected the heavenly, the earth reacted
to man. Babel represented the seeking of lost humanity to
reconnect with the heavens, albeit rebelliously. Until they
and we do reconnect, we cannot dwell or abide in the land,
but will wander over across the face of it, lacking roots, depth
and permanence as a living sign that we lack eternity. That is
why defilement will cause the land to *'vomit out its inhabitants'* (Leviticus 18:25 NKJV). The land itself resonates with
heaven that these things should not be and are to be rejected.
Sin must not be allowed to take root and become permanent,
even eternal. Angels with flaming swords are positioned
against this happening. But the land is completed by humankind, and made for them, so without a right relationship
with them, the land suffers neglect and '... *the anxious longing of the creation waits eagerly for the revealing of the sons of God
... For we know that the whole creation groans and suffers the*

*pains of childbirth together until now'* (Romans 8:19, 22). Restored relationship with heavenly reality must issue in restored and new relationship with the land.

How then should we relate, as children in restored relationship with our Heavenly Father, living and moving in the unseen realms of the spiritual places, to the seen and tangible land of our Europe? No longer ignorantly of the spiritual realities that affect the very earth beneath our feet. No longer glibly about the blood spilt, the wars fought, the injustices perpetrated on this piece of creation destined for glory and crying out for restitution. No longer casually or despisingly of decay or abuse. No longer pragmatically. Now we have to embrace the land, the history of the particular territory, the human experience expressed and sown into this dust. Now we have to pray for it, repent over it for the unresolved bloodguilt and the barriers, borders and divisions to which the land itself does not witness. Now we have to groan with it, intercede for its healing and draw up its hidden inheritance. Now we have to priest it and all the peoples it represents. Now we have to read the signs it prophesies and respond accordingly.

## Covenant

The land of Europe itself is agreeing with heaven in the groaning and longing for the sons of God, the Church, to be revealed. The Church of God is known in the Spirit by covenant. On earth she may be known by certain behaviour, but in truth she is established by covenant.

> *'I am God Almighty; walk before me and be blameless. And I will establish My covenant between Me and you...'*
> (Genesis 17:1–2)

God makes a covenant with people, a binding commitment. He always takes the initiative, but He asks for a response for that covenant to be established. And, not surprisingly in the light of all we have just discussed, when

God first made a covenant with Abram, it was in the context of the land, because covenant with God is eternal in nature. We should become rooted and re-established in right relationship with the created order as we are established in the heavens.

> *'And I will establish my covenant between Me and you ...*
> *for an everlasting covenant, to be God to you and to your*
> *descendants after you. And I will give to you ... all the land*
> *... for an everlasting possession.'*          (Genesis 17:7–8)

It is because of this eternal connection with the God of all creation that a binding love commitment to Him invokes in us and requires from us also a binding commitment to the land of our dwelling. This is why Isaiah can use the term of marriage to the land. Speaking of Israel, the land and the people are talked of as one:

> *'It will no longer be said to you, "Forsaken,"*
> *Nor to your land will it any longer be said, "Desolate";*
> *But you will be called "My delight is in her,"*
> *And your land, "Married";*
> *For the Lord delights in you,*
> *And to Him your land will be married.'*          (Isaiah 62:4)

The experience of John Mulinde in Uganda is a telling illustration of discovery of this truth. His binding commitment to God led him to groan with identificational grief for his nation. It was not enough for this non-European to settle for individual salvation. His salvation merely established him in covenant with the God of heaven and earth and located him into the experience of his land and his nation, in his feelings, loves, desires and guilt. As he groaned and expressed the grief of the land for the loss and injustice, the pain and disgrace of many years, the Lord began to speak to him of covenant, and of John entering into a covenant with God for the land of Uganda. If he would bind his life from God to the land, it would be as if he could bind the whole land of

Uganda back to God via his own bond of covenant. This was no light thing! It was accompanied with deep intercession, with fasting and due seriousness. So with the involvement of 300 other leaders of similar commitment, the whole land of Uganda has been blessed, the physical land as well as the spheres of life in government, trade and social organisation. Now God has led John to make the same covenant, the same binding commitment, to see the salvation and redemption of Europe. We need to receive this grace and light from our brother. If he can hear that the revelation of the sons of God is marked in covenant and make such a sacrificial commitment to our lands, should not we who are created from this European dust be likewise faithful? Should not we also be answering the cries of our land, that Europe be married to the King of kings and no longer prostituted to false gods and unclean lifestyle?

## An Interpretative Narrative

The narrative of the book of Ruth offers great insight for us at such a time as this in Europe. It begins with the land prophesying that all is not well! Even the land that God has chosen to make a sign in the earth of His covenant and grace to people is suffering famine. There is no bread in Bethlehem, the house of bread. In the land that was known for the promises of God there is no fruit, and the people are wandering from their land. Death and loss follow until Naomi has nowhere to turn but back to the promises. She is humbled. *'Do not call me fruitful, but call me bitter'* (1:20). There is no clearer picture of Christian Europe. Now old, with memories of past glories fading but past the ability to bear new life, grieving, disappointed, where can we go except to humble repentance, ready to turn our face back towards our land and our promises? At this point a Ruth rises up to make a wonderfully sacrificial choice and covenant! A different generation, a different nation, free to go back and make a new start according to the flesh, she chooses instead to covenant to the old lady and to the hope of a new day.

How we should thank God for the sacrificial prayer and reconciliation of the nations of the earth, turning back to old Europe in a time of our loss! How awesome that the hearts of the children of the gospel are turning back to us, to commit with us to hope again.

On their return to Bethlehem, it is at the beginning of the barley harvest and Ruth becomes the support to her mother-in-law. The famine is beginning to be over, although not essentially for Naomi who would not be able to benefit from the changing season due to her former loss. Pause, and think on that! But Ruth takes the initiative and goes gleaning in the fields. We have said much about the sacrifice and vulnerability of those God is calling to Europe to come and help us and will say more. We owe them due honour and should be humble and grateful enough to receive from them, to glean from their faith and experience of God's presence and grace. For Ruth did have a terrific revelation of grace. Boaz, as the picture of Christ, hears of her sacrifice and her covenant and immediately starts to make provision and protection available to her. There is grain, wine and water for her and Naomi and a strong word that she should be safe.

But now Naomi rises up and encourages Ruth to press in further. She adds her faith and relationship to the equation and urges Ruth to a new level of covenant. Naomi begins to look beyond the salvation and provision of the present moment to the possibility of a **completely new** arrangement. She sees that the former way of living and receiving God's blessing and provision was good, but there is an even higher calling. With hindsight on this little Old Testament book, we are seeing God transitioning His people from one level of experience to a quite other one. Judges have been and gone and the nation is rising a little here, falling back a little, now settling. But God's purpose is greater! This little nation of Israel is not called just to survive, nor even be blessed, but to become a sign and wonder of how God's marvellous reign and rule can break into the earth! No longer do we need the occasional judge to sort out the nation, but David must come forth to shine into the world! So when

Naomi rallies and allies herself with Ruth, she is calling for the future redemptive purpose of all that was lost. Not just restored, but fulfilled! Ruth, become a bride, not just a servant! Take off the old clothes of lost identity and marginalisation and go for something new! Wash yourself and put on your best clothes! Approach as a bride, a lover, a partner! Approach and ask for that to which you are not entitled.

Now, as a picture of what God is doing in Europe, we believe this is a real challenge to us. For Naomi and Ruth to reach out together for something so much greater than anything they had before, they will have to risk everything of their present level of favour and comfort. Ruth herself, though so gracious and given, can only expect to reach the level that Naomi would expect. After all, Naomi is the steward of the promises of God. Ruth has only received that which came from Naomi. So it may be with the children of the gospel and empire as we have said. Their faith, energy and humility are a challenge and glory to revive and encourage us. But their paradigm will likely always only be that which they received. If we have learned nothing from the loss and captivity of our history, nor will they, and the third day process of the gospel will follow the pattern of the second day as surely as winter follows summer. The structural and corporate demonisation that eventually attacked and overcame the glorious waves of revival in this continent will follow and destroy the subsequent waves even to the ends of the earth. Unless the old lady who has been embittered but humbled can receive not just hope for a new filling of this continent with God's glory but a vision for a new form to contain it! Unless we can find faith and courage to go beyond revival and see what else needs to changed and challenged in order to fully redeem Europe's calling to receive and manifest the Kingdom of God into the earth. When Naomi finally arose in partnership with Ruth, she went beyond the hope of comfort and ease, right through to a vision of a new covenant, and eternal destiny, not just for her and her family, but for the nation and, through it, the nations of the world. She was willing and urgent to invest her present hope and comfort into a potentially totally new order! At the time of threshing, she allowed her motives and expectations to be threshed. At the time of winnowing, she submitted her mindsets and paradigms to be judged. She and Ruth went for broke! We believe the European Church is ready to risk all for a new day.

## So What of the Land?

The book of Ruth is a book about covenant. In the first chapter Ruth speaks out a seven-fold covenant in which she 'cleaved to' Naomi. In the second chapter Boaz encourages Ruth to cleave to his maidservants and, by chapter 3, this cleaving has become 'lying down to' or submitting in total surrender to Boaz. We are familiar with the need to be in covenant, surrendered relationship to Christ, as pictured here by Boaz, and we understand, though perhaps practise less often, the same need to be in surrendered relationships to others in the body of Christ, as in the reconciliation between Naomi and Ruth. Being covenanted, wholly committed to a servant model of leadership, taking initiative at whatever cost to serve others while not demanding that anyone recognise or submit to us, is a lesson we should learn from Ruth in chapter 2 as she gave herself to that and invoked the strong approval and protection of Boaz in so doing.

But between chapters 3 and 4 there is a lull. It is a poignant and costly moment, a moment of opportunity and potential, but also great danger. Sound familiar? The mixture and disorder of past covenants broken by death, relationships changed, hopes kindled, legal claims and human choices come to a climax. And it all focuses on the issue of the ownership of land in the light of covenant. Though Boaz is smitten with his lovely bride and she with him there is to be no consummation of this joyous love without resolving the issue of her inheritance. There is another who has right of inheritance over the land because of the death of Elimelech (which means 'My God is King') and his sons. This other one has a present claim on the land because of the loss of the true authority in it. But here comes Ruth, who some would consider a nobody, an alien and stranger, but who is carrying a covenantal (by her former marriage) relationship to the land. Suddenly there is a challenge to the one who has legal right to buy the land. Ruth's desire to make a new covenant with Boaz requires him to release his right to her inheritance because the covenanted land must follow her other covenants. Equally, if he will not release the land, then because she has a covenantal link to the land, he must also receive her when he takes possession of the land. The covenant with the land is inviolable. Where she belongs, it comes. Or where it is owned, she must go.

This is true priesthood. Ruth is offered up, by the one who is the image of Christ, who loves her and to whom she is given, as a sacrificial offering for the sake of an inheritance! Is this really how the Lord would treat His Church? Yes, if she would be willing. For the Lord loves everything that He has made and was willing to die for all people to be saved and for the whole of creation to be redeemed. Without covenantal authority at work in the land, it is reduced to fallen material earth. As such men and women have legal right to treat it and view it as such. The corollary is that the one to whom fallen men and women are consciously or unconsciously covenanted can also make legal claim on the earth to build strongholds and fortresses for evil which then infect and disease those who come and live there. Remember, territory precedes inhabiting it. But if the bride is mature enough to choose to abandon herself to another man, the new man, in whom righteous authority is restored, this maturity provokes a challenge to the legal but unworthy claim! Now notice the genius of the challenge to the nearer kinsman in this story, he who represents the flesh or the natural, or in some ways by process of unrighteous covenants, the prince of this world. Whether by receiving Ruth in marriage to assert his legal right to the land, or by rejecting her and giving up his right, this usurper loses the land! For should she marry him, her children will inherit it. His claim is doomed to only one more generation at best and, even then, he might find that they gain all his other possessions as well! It's a lose/lose scenario and he loses!

For the Church to be a worthy partner and growing increasingly into the image of the one she loves, she will be ready to embrace this kind of priesthood for all that and all those who are not yet in right relationship with Him. Jesus offered Himself up for the sake of that which was lost and calls those who would be His disciples to *'take up your cross and follow'* (Matthew 16:24). If we are covenanted to the Lord, established in relationship to Him by life or by death, we have nothing to lose except our full calling and destiny if we do not also re-establish covenant with our land. But as we mature in our love and passion for our Lord Jesus and recognise the scope of all that God wants to redeem in Him, we will also hear the cry of the land and be reconciled in a priestly relationship with it. No longer to wander across the face of the land, we will re-establish a covenant with God for the city, territory, nation or continent to which He is connecting us, and whether by life or by death, we will embrace it in the same covenant by which we are bonded to the heavens. Then, and only then, we will drag it from its present captivity into its destined glory! Then and only then, we will draw up and receive the power of all the grace and anointing laid down in the land both by creation and by the prophetic lives and sacrifice, the prayers and servanthood of those who have gone before. Then and only then, we will provoke the usurper to yield and give up our inheritance! Let's do it!

## *Chapter 6*

# Reformed to Refill All Things!

God is speaking clearly to His European peoples. He is addressing captive mindsets and dislocation in all its manifestations. He is doing a work of the same order and significance as the first reformation in Europe. And His purpose is to line us all up, to reconcile all things to the blood of Christ. He is realigning the Church with the land and, through it, with all of creation and addressing the divide between her and those to whom He is sending her. Through years of difficulty, He has trained and proved us, fed us and prepared us, ready to sow us afresh into our nations. But we believe there is now a key moment of adjustment, ready for this sowing which is necessary to bring about a fresh harvest in our continent.

We looked earlier at the original content and nature of the gospel, the gospel of the Kingdom, and then we looked at the land, with its different shapes, peoples and cultures and the way in which this affects both the perception and the reception of the gospel. It becomes clear then that for the gospel of the Kingdom to reach into the land, the role and the nature of the vehicle that carries it is key. This is the Church, the people of God and the agent of the Kingdom.

Two things immediately stand out. The first is that this vehicle will have to be much more flexible and adaptable in order to make effective connections into all the different contexts and circumstances that the fullness and complexity of creation now constitutes. Second, it will need to be much better attuned to the nature of the gospel itself, in order not to be counter-intuitive to the expression of God's freely given love and grace. River beds mould themselves to the water and the water flows inexorably where it wills. But concrete canals limit and control the water and it risks becoming diverted from its original course or, worse still, stagnant. Further, shapes or vehicles that are themselves formed by and for controlling, dominant or oppressive ends carry their own taint which pollutes anything that is carried by that vehicle. We are all well acquainted with the phenomenon of how politicians in particular seem to change after they have sat in the seat of power for any length of time. It is as if the very structure, seat or office has a personality of its own which begins to impact the new incumbent. We would be foolish to imagine that this does not also happen to 'Christian' structures. As we have said, we have borrowed the shape and practice of much of our church organisation from the empires of previous generations. The imperial spirit has infected many of our expressions of Church, and needs exorcising. New forms and organisation that react proudly or dismissively to the old ways themselves also often corrupt by their very reactions! When there was death in the river, Elisha instructed the prophets to take a *'new bowl and put salt in it'* (2 Kings 2:20 NKJV). At this point in church development, we need loads of new bowls, formed out of old and new materials, but which will all need filling with preservative, shaping and offering up to God, ready for a new season.

So what might be the structures and shapes that God wants to form in Europe for such a time as this? Given that God has so used the European nations to discover and open up hidden lands and fill them with the gospel, it is likely that our redemptive purpose is to do so again. But this time, so help us God, we will have been so remoulded, so humbled by our failures, that we will be able to learn from how we fell back from or even prostituted this gift and calling and be restored to design and develop new skills, practice and shapes that God can marvellously fill with new hidden treasures from out of the darkness. We thank God too for the encourage-ment and insight from those of our friends from the third day Church who, with the vibrant strength of the gospel still rushing in the river beds of their lands, are able to help us, as we also remember the poignant question of our young Korean friend, longing and desperate that the now maturing river in his land would not become silted up and siphoned off into stagnant pools.

## Standing Together

We are being called back to inhabit our lands. We find it extraordinary how concerned God is for creation, even to the point that He speaks to her and prophesies to her:

> *'Thus says the Lord God to the mountains and to the hills, to the ravines and to the valleys, to the desolate wastes and to the forsaken cities, which have become a prey and a derision to the rest of the nations which are round about ... Therefore prophesy concerning the land of Israel ... For, behold, I am for you ... and you shall be cultivated and sown...'* (Ezekiel 36:4, 6, 9)

Remember Israel is our father and our teacher. What pertains between the people of Israel and their land is given to us for a sign and example for all the nations to learn from. Here there is no harvest, no blessing and no spiritual fruitfulness in the land from which, in every sphere of creation, the people of God have been removed. Whether as here, by physical exile, or whether as today in Europe where we as the Church have largely withdrawn from our priestly authoritative role in culture and society, government or education, or in consistent assertive prayer for our whole land, the land suffers from the lack of the revelation of the children of God. And this is the very context for the Ezekiel passages we know so well. In the face of this decay in the land, God takes the initiative to bring His people back to the land, and this not because of their rights or merit, but because of the shame such a situation brings on His own name. So firstly He promises that He will *'give you a new heart and put a new spirit within you; and I will remove the heart of stone from your flesh and give you a heart of flesh. And I will put My Spirit within you and cause you to walk in My statutes and you will be careful to observe My ordinances. And you will live in the land . . . '* (Ezekiel 36:26–28). A restored and vital flow of heavenly life in and through the people of God is the number one requirement. Thank God for His initiatives throughout the centuries in our lands and the marvellous signs of His refreshing and refilling us again today for another great thrust forward.

This is to lead us to new levels of holiness, and this again in the context of a harvest in the land and an end to famine. In such a context, the Lord must be speaking about corporate sin, since land always represents the corporate life of a nation. He encourages us to *'remember your deeds that were not good'* (Ezekiel 36:31). It is a time for due consideration and priestly repentance of past unresolved corporate attitudes and behaviour, to come into a higher level of effectiveness. When this is in order, He promises that the *'desolate land will be cultivated . . . And they will say, "This desolate land has become like the garden of Eden; and the waste, desolate and ruined cities are fortified and inhabited"'* (Ezekiel 36:34, 35). This is our dream and our longing.

So how does the Lord structure His people to achieve this goal in the land? He has to speak to dry bones and change them into a living, mighty army that stands in the land! There can be no doubt either from this passage or from the many words, prophecies and signs of these present times, that the only way for the Church to be reformed for this moment is in a new and effective experience of unity. Rick Joyner writes,

> 'Ultimately the unity of the church in the midst of . . . worldwide discord will be the marvel of the world and the greatest testimony ever of the Lordship of Jesus. However this power will be very subtle as first. It will

touch hearts deeply but few will even discuss what they are pondering in their hearts because of their fears.'

(Mobilizing the Army of God,<br>Morning Star publications, 1994)

Every Christian knows that unity is essential to pleasing God, to functioning effectively and to power. Many have therefore sought it hungrily, but up until now it has mainly only been possible to achieve certain levels of heart relationship among those with whom we have a great deal in common in our theology, ecclesiology or, more usually, our generation. But Ezekiel's vision is clearly interpreted for us as the very many, very dry bones scattered across the face of the valley representing *'the **whole** house of Israel; behold, they say, "Our bones are dried up and our hope has perished. We are completely cut off* [lit. to ourselves]*"'* (Ezekiel 37:11).

## The Gift of Facilitation

Now deep relationships between many different types and backgrounds of people who all name the name of Jesus and share His life is not an easy thing to attempt. Like Ezekiel, were the Lord to ask us if we think this can be accomplished we would have to say, 'Oh Lord, you know!' It can and will only be achieved by the flow of the new heart, new spirit that the Lord has promised us. We are not referring to a structural or formal attempt to bring all church leaders, for example, together into one room and expect a unity to manifest! There is the need for the hand of the Lord to bring someone, or ideally a central core of two or three together as one, to stand in the middle of the valley to prophesy, to see what as yet no one else can see, that relationship and open friendship can and must happen and be extended. The hand or grace of the Lord in this situation manifests as a new gift of leadership. It is a leadership that facilitates others and is able to put them at their ease. There can be nothing to be gained for this person but dying and rejection, like Ezekiel, like Jesus. Because Joyner is right in his assessment. It is deep-seated fear that keeps us back but it is this fear and discord that is losing us a huge battle. There is so much to risk in drawing closer to those different in their expression of faith and this has to be managed by sacrificial time, visits, prayer, sensitive gifts, hospitality and listening. But there is so much more to risk if we do not grasp this nettle.

If the body of the Lord is dismembered, it will never stand in the land. Roger Forster, a senior leader in the Charismatic movement, who taught us so much from his deep grasp of the Word and church history, made a remarkable historical observation in the pamphlet *Spiritual Warfare in Church History* (Ichthus Media Services, 1997). It illustrates vividly the result of not being connected to one another, to the Lord and to the land. Consider the seventy years of the exile of the Lord's people Israel, when they were physically removed from the territory to which they were covenanted. Among the centuries of their history, it's a blink of an eye. Yet in that very same, specific period of relatively few years a phenomenon occurred around the world. All the major monistic religions with the exception of Sikhism had their origins in that period of time. Seemingly unrelated to each other, the early shoots of Hinduism, Buddhism and Confucianism all appeared in that 'window of opportunity'. It is a remarkable corollary and one which should deeply challenge us. When we are displaced, the enemy of souls can let rip! But if we who are reconciled to Christ will reconcile with each other and stand in right order and authority in the creation, we can keep the enemy's deceptions under our feet.

In the experience of the Argentinean revival, the leaders in a city strategise together to this end. At great cost, in the trauma of the unjust military junta in power in their land, men like Omar Cabrera and Ed Silvoso worked to build unity among the church leaders in the cities. The stories of towns such as Resistencia and San Nicolas are now well known. Drawing on these experiences, Ed has written the strategy down. He describes how unity in a territory is a key factor in 'causing Satan to fall down' in that place, so that the spiritual climate changes, the revelation of the gospel gains a new access and justice and healing can be restored. Research into the places in the earth where the growth of the gospel and the blessing of the people and the land itself have improved measurably always highlights the depth, and the cost, of heart unity among leaders of God's people. The video compilations *Transformations 1* and *II* is one such resource of documentary evidence.

## City Shaped Land

If we are looking towards the unity of the body of Christ relating to the land, we have to look at the importance of cities in expressing the life and intensity of communities located in creation. Though the biblical narrative begins with people and God in a garden, with the result that our view of creation is usually informed by the rural idyll, the city is the first manifestation of humanity expressing itself outside of the garden, which God planted. It seems at first to be a rebellious and unworthy creation of Cain, in direct contradiction to God setting him wandering on the face of the earth. But Cain had already cried, *'My punishment is too great to bear!'* (Genesis 4:13), and his fear and pleading won a reprieve from the Lord who marked him for mercy. So it says that *'he settled in the land of wandering'* (Genesis 4:16). The settlement became a sign of a city of refuge, a halfway house back from judgement. In a few generations the city of Enoch was established and when Eve conceived again and received Seth as a restoration sign for the loss of Abel, the Scripture records that *'Then men began to call upon the name of the Lord'* (Genesis 4:26). From this point on God recognises and works with city structure, even to the point of choosing a city as His bride!

Here in the establishment of the first city there is a lovely four-fold image of the spheres of human life in relationship with the created order. For the basic building block of community is family and human relationships. Cain took a wife, had a son and named the city after him. Social shapes and interaction function as crucial components of our creation experience, reflected in this city. Much could be said about how today's cities in Europe are having to take full account of this again in the way that family and social need rather than economics should affect architecture, schooling, support structures, but for the moment we are simply describing the broadest spheres of city reality. We go on to read of three other activities in this city. There is *'Jabal ... the father of those who dwell in tents and have livestock'* (Genesis 4:20). Part of our creation mandate is fruitfulness, provision and interaction with the agricultural processes necessary to life and health. Cities, in their concentrated representation of human activity, are not supposed to be separated from the very land itself and the biblical image of city always has its hinterland in mind. It is very poignant for us to be writing this while Britain is in the grip of a very serious outbreak of Foot and Mouth Disease in the national flock. As an exercise in indifference for the average city dweller it was remarkable! For the farmers it was devastating. The divorce between rural and urban life is shocking and destructive. Natural creation is our template and context for creativity and without interaction with it, we risk an easy descent into barren utilitarianism.

> *'And his brother's name was Jubal; he was the father of all those who play the lyre and the pipe.'*        (Genesis 4:21)

Culture, imagination, music and artistic expression and communication of emotions, dreams, and aspirations are clearly part of our God-breathed humanity. It is the expression of our ability not only to subdue, but also to be fruitful, civilising and comforting. And his half-brother was Tubal-Cain, *'the forger of all implements of bronze and iron'* (Genesis 4:22). Here is industry, strength and dominion. Here is wealth creation, invention and struggle. Such are the contrasts, gifts, potential and glories of our cities where our God wants to dwell with, in and through us.

So this is the shape of our present land, and the shape of the gospel is of the Kingdom of God. In such a Kingdom,

His rule will be expressed and its effects experienced in human relationships and interaction. Where things are out of order, they will need re-ordering and disciplining, and communication about all this with the source of it will therefore be essential. This is why the essence of early church life was the apostles' teaching (the definition, culture and proclamation of His rule), fellowship (as it is expressed, shared and incarnated by His images), breaking of bread (the place of merciful resolution of discord and disorder) and prayer (communication and new instructions for implementation)! Now, how to match these essentials to the city shape?

## Church at the Interface

Firstly, the Church will need to be positioned throughout all the spheres. Truth is, she almost certainly already is, but not consciously. Members of the body of Christ generally think of themselves as such only when they are gathered together in one place with the rest of the members. (Truth is, here also there is an unhelpful perception. Only some of the members of the body are gathered in that particular local gathering. A missing arm, three toes, an elbow and six vertebrae are scattered around in other buildings in town!) Now there are two parables about the nature of Church, the agent of the Kingdom, in the Scriptures (see Mark 4). The first we know very well. It is about the seed, which is the word of God coming to us, and as we work with it in our understanding (the hardened path), past personal experiences (where rocks of stumbling may lurk), desires and ambitions (where weeds of covetousness or fear may grow), it begins to bear good fruit in our lives. That is why we come together to be taught, healed up, to be disciplined by the word and one another, in order to become fruitful. This is important for the carriers of Kingdom life, the Church. We must be sure that we have received and grown the fruit and reality of the Kingdom in our own lives, and none of us are really ever confident that we have done that enough! But the second parable is also about seed and is connected to the first. It flows straight on seamlessly in Jesus' teaching, although they are rarely heard taught together in church! This is where a man takes good seed and sows it in his field. This good seed is the sons of the Kingdom, obviously those who have multiplied the seed of the word in their own lives as in the first parable! Now we are no longer in receiving mode, but in scattered mode! Now we don't pluck up the wheat and tares, the people who so far have given in to the cares and covetousness, but grow tall and straight among them in an alternate lifestyle. Now we look forward to a harvest as *'the seed whose fruit is righteousness is sown in peace'* (James 3:18).

## Every Member

Every member of the Church has got to get the mindset that they are seed for the field as well as ground in the Church. It's an identity issue, not just a confidence issue. This is why the good seed has come to us, to form us into great planting seed! True, for many Christians it is a confidence issue, but you know, even weak seed, once it's planted, can draw more strength from the land itself. But longer on the stem at harvest time will not help it to grow any further. It is also a leadership issue. Teachers and leaders have got to find ways in which to thrust the people away from them, rather than gathering them inwards. But this threatens our own role and identity. Perhaps our willingness to die first in this transition from one identity to another will break something open for others and mark true leadership.

Then every member of the Church should try and identify which sphere of the created order, of the city, they are called to or positioned in. For some this will be an exercise of heart, for others a pragmatic consideration of which job they do or where they spend the most time. Either is valid. Where am I planted? This is the land that I covenant to. As an individual carrier of the Kingdom, here is where it can and will grow. But how can I promote that growth?

## The Apostles' Teaching

Ed Silvoso calls himself an implementer, and his strategic seminars on how to activate every member of the body of Christ in this process of reaching a whole city give extremely clear, practical insights into biblical teaching. He draws attention to the process of Luke 10 where Jesus sends out His Kingdom agents, and in particular to the order. He points out that speaking peace to a situation precedes declaration or proclamation of any other kind. Now if we remember the core values of the Kingdom, this makes every sense. To be devoted to the apostles' teaching is not only to receive and obey it, but to promote and speak it. Scattered seed is sent out. As we embrace our 'scattered' identity, we are embracing an apostolic call and ministry. We are sent out into creation from the hand of the Father and carrying His life. Therefore we can prophesy, speak blessing, not just as a prayer but as a powerful act that the Father will affirm. We are sent out to open up new opportunities for God's Kingdom and there is some groundwork to be done before we necessarily get massive breakthrough. Speaking out peace, declaring the love that the Father has for this sphere of creation that He has called into being and loves enough to position one of His agents there, begins to contest the darkness and change the balance of spiritual authority. It is apostolic teaching to the principalities and powers and can and should be in the mouth of every Christian who is cast, apostled, into the land!

## Fellowship

Then in Luke 10 Jesus encourages His followers to eat with and accept hospitality from those to whom they are sent. Fellowship is also the key second factor of Kingdom lifestyle. But surely fellowship refers to the heart relationship we have with other believers? We would call it fellowship that Jesus shared with the Samaritan women when He sat down tired at the well and asked her to draw some water for Him. It certainly was by the end of the encounter! If the tide is turning and the Lord is changing the time from a gathering of His people to one side to be taught to a season of thrusting them out to be teachers, it is a time of initiative for the people of God. If we have truly received the flow of His life and are given to His world, we should no longer be afraid to open ourselves to those living in idolatry and darkness. Light is stronger than darkness and love stronger than death. In the Old Testament, the priests went through major ritual to become ceremonially clean, but if their clean garments touched death or impurity, they immediately became unclean again. But when Jesus came, truly clean and pure, He touched the leper. The flow was immediately reversed and the clean made the unclean clean! When we lived overseas, our landlords were a delightful Indian family. The mother of the family particularly was a very devout Hindu who often participated in ritual suffering, walking on hot coals and piercing her face with large metal spikes. We longed for her to taste the grace and healing of God which would save her from this need to deal so dreadfully with her own guilt and fears. We invited them to eat with us, but they were too shy. We greeted them daily, prayed for them fervently but got no nearer until their festival of Diwali. This is when every Indian family makes huge amounts of food and is religiously bound to share it with strangers and the poor. Now we were poor! But this was food specifically offered to idols (which was probably what they had thought about ours and why they had resisted our hospitality). Sue admits to being reluctant but Roger knew the Scriptures allowed us to eat it, so visit them we did. Crouching on their little balcony, we celebrated Diwali with our hands in the communal bowl of deliciously scented rice and tasted all manner of delicacy. My mouth still waters at the memory! From then on, our landlady began to teach Sue the finer art of cooking such dishes. A few months later when their grandson became suddenly, dangerously ill, the Hindu priest wouldn't come and a doctor was out of the question, our landlady pleaded with us to pray for the little boy, and the Lord raised him up. Since Jesus commanded it, we can all aspire to and pray for opportunities to fellowship with not-yet-believers on their terms rather than ours.

## Breaking of Bread

'And heal those in the city who are sick' is the next instruction that Jesus gives to those He is scattering. Ed Silvoso would interpret this to mean that we should pray for and meet the felt needs of those we are covenanted to in our 'land'. This is a Kingdom lifestyle. When Jesus died in our place, He acted according to our real, felt need. We needed deliverance and mercy, so He stood in the place of our judgement and death to release us at great cost to Himself. Whenever we celebrate the breaking of bread, we are remembering and receiving this fantastic, over the top, gloriously unreasonable exchange of life for death! And this is what we have to live out in the land. Living in a fallen environment, often to our shame as much in church as anywhere else, we should by now be well practised at knowing how to deal with criticism and rejection, with jealousy and backbiting. And apparently it is not by up-fronting it and demanding justice! Jesus said to us to turn the other cheek, not to return evil for evil but to overcome evil with good. We are the wheat growing up among tares and manifesting different fruit. In the circumstances of our living, moving and having our being, we must develop the habit of returning blessing for cursing, our own death for someone else's life. Some years ago we felt that some colleagues had seriously sinned against us. The mixture of anger and resentment could easily have turned to bitterness. But the Lord showed us that the key was for us to break bread together, repenting of any sin we had done and forgiving the sin done against us. This we did daily and deliberately for several months. The breaking of bread is, as we have already seen in Chapter 4, more than a memorial sign and thanksgiving but a prophetic act that releases the Kingdom of God powerfully into our specific situation. In this way it is an active and potent weapon of spiritual war. In situations where cities and nations have been polluted by past sin and bloodshed we have similarly found that repentance and the breaking of bread has released the power of the cross and brought cleansing and forgiveness to the land. There are numerous examples of this, some of which are recorded in *The Sins of the Fathers* (Sovereign, 1999). We need to break bread much more often than most of us do. It seems clear from the New Testament that the practice of breaking bread from house to house was as normal for Christians as saying grace before meals is today. The release of the presence of the Kingdom into our homes and meal times would have a huge impact on the spiritual climate. Nor should we be afraid to do this at the right moment even when not-yet-Christians are present. The release of the presence and power of God will bring the Kingdom of God near. Most people's felt need is for the miracle of love and acceptance. Most people's inner need is for peace and belonging. Some will be ready to participate and the communion will be for them the consummation of the act of repentance. For others, if we explain sensitively what our practice means, just to watch and be present will manifest the presence of God to them. It is showing forth the compassion of Jesus, and if we can offer this, then the healing miracles, the financial provision, the employment, the practical signs of God's intervention will be easy things to accomplish by prayer. Of course, it will not always be appropriate to break bread literally and publicly. Many times it is the meaning and heart attitude of the cross that we will demonstrate by laying our own lives down into a situation of need. Carlos Annacondia, a man of small physical stature but immense spiritual grace, who has led literally millions of people to Christ, seen amazing healings and extraordinary miracles in stadium campaigns throughout Argentina as well as internationally, speaks so gently and soul-piercingly about the source of power ministry. Speaking of the Lord, he draws out the word 'compassion' from the Scriptures. It is the Father's love in Him that sourced the power of Jesus' life. At the most basic but truly significant level, it is when the individual Christian, working in say, a newspaper office, knowing he or she is there as an agent of the Kingdom of God, who when asked to work late because of someone else's laziness, does so. And while doing so, he or she blesses and prays for both the lazy irresponsible colleague and the over-bearing, unreasonable boss. This is the one who is releasing the power of the breaking of bread into the sphere of creation! This is the one who, when the unreasonable boss's marriage comes under pressure (because it would not be easy to be married to him!), will be able to pray for a change, to share the secret of repentance and forgiveness! Meeting people's felt needs in the light of the breaking of bread and what it stands for is the gospel of the Kingdom. Some would call it foolish. Christians should not allow themselves to be made use of. These people need to understand justice and fairness. And we are presumably the ones to teach them? The breaking of bread that we participate in is, from our point of view as sinners, not at all about justice and fairness! It is about extraordinary love and sacrifice that overcomes evil with unreasonable goodness! There will be many reading this who are responding angrily. They will want to keep a private feast. But we want *'to proclaim the Lord's death until He comes'* (1 Corinthians 11:26).

## And Prayer

The prayers of the early Church were those that built bridges between heaven and earth. That is why, in Luke 10, Jesus could instruct His resistance army to go and *'say to* [those in the city], *"The kingdom of God has come near to you."'* The prayers of this apostled church member will be the key to connecting the land of his or her calling to the heavenly places of his or her belonging. The disciples finally learnt this and immediately after this first foray into the open spaces of creation calling to be inseminated with the love of God, they return rejoicing, but ready to be taught the business of prayer. Once they have been given and received the respons-ibility to go and be the seed, the salt, the change agents, then they learn to pray!

The point is this: God is looking for the activation of every born-again person as an agent of His Kingdom, ready or not, because the land is calling for the revelation of the children of God. The gospel of the Kingdom is flowing irrevocably into every sphere of the city and the land, flowing through every Christian speaking blessing, deeply and sacrificially loving and praying. We do not need to prepare people long and hard to succeed in this. Rick Joyner writes of future leaders,

> 'One of the primary reasons the church today is so weak and so un-prepared for the times is not under-preparation but **over-preparation**. We are requiring our future leaders to be much more than what God requires because we do not trust the Holy Spirit enough ... We will have to give them more and more responsibility with increasingly less training. The Holy Spirit will make up the difference and that will make these leaders some of the greatest the world has ever known. His strength is still made perfect in weakness.'
>
> (*Mobilizing the Army of God*,
> Morning Star publications, 1994)

This is a time for future leaders to appear now, every agent of the Kingdom leading the land into wholeness.

## Two or Threes

It is the power of unity that the Lord is emphasising at the same time. So there will be agreements forming where the sphere of life, be it the health services of a particular city or the clubbing scene of Saturday night, determines the composition of the 'church'. Where two or three are gathered in Jesus' name, He comes to agree with them and make His presence felt. As two or three agents recognise the Spirit of Jesus in each other and a common commitment to take responsibility for releasing Kingdom life into this creation, they will be being 'church'. Increasingly such groups or cells are forming in businesses, or in areas of town where several similar businesses are grouped together and Kingdom agents are meeting to pray, worship and support one another in the particular stresses related to that sphere of life. It is and will increasingly become more than a 'Christian union' meeting for Bible study and prayer or even evangelism. Remember, God is rekindling the heart. Meetings without forming deep relationships are going nowhere. Deep relationships in prayer and common concern for invading spheres of society are functioning church. This will lead to inevitable questions about loyalty to 'the church' by which we normally mean the local congregation to which people usually belong. Where is this Kingdom person's primary commitment? What about accountability? Does he or she have the pastor's blessing? Does he or she need it? Does the local pastor have any jurisdiction in this new group and how will that work out if all the pastors of the members of the group want a say? The questions are endless but all have to do with the nature of what is 'real' church and the nature of who is in charge of what!

## Apostolic Forms of Church

As we already made clear in Chapter 4, our biblical exegesis and theology needs to be based on the gospels or, to put it another way, must be incarnational. This also applies to our understanding of the way we express church. We have already considered the fact that church is generic, something you are once you receive and commit to the revelation that Jesus is the Christ. We saw too that the Lord spoke of church and explained how to deal with disputes between disciples by 'telling it to the church' long before the church had any geographical expression (cf. Matthew 18:17). We must conclude from this that the original expression of church structure was in fact the apostolic band of twelve gathered around the Lord, with its inner core of three. This was expressed further in the teams of two that the Lord sent out both from the twelve and from the seventy. It's an interesting possibility, although at best a guess from the gospel account, that the seventy, also described as seventy-two, were the product of the six pairs that the twelve went out in. Assuming that they themselves looked for groups of twelve to disciple it would explain where the seventy-two came from! What is for sure is that groups of twelve carry a Kingdom dynamic that Jesus confirmed and empowered. This explains at least in part the success of cell churches that build on this Christ-inspired dynamic which we do well to recognise and adapt to the new shapes of church that the Holy Spirit leads us into. However, whether or not the latter process happened, the main point here is that the original expression of church was a travelling band, not a locally-based community of believers. This is born out by apostolic practice in the Acts of the Apostles. In fact it is an obvious point that we sometimes forget, that without the apostolic forms of church there would be no local ones. The apostolic form expresses foundational apostolic work, taking new territory, or we suggest, recovering old territory. It seems from the Lord's original strategy and the subsequent mission-ary practice of the apostles, that bands travelling throughout a region or nation create the impact and spiritual climate change that can then be consolidated and built on from a significant geographical location such as a capital city like Jerusalem. At times of loss, transition and recovery like we are currently going through in Europe there is great need for these apostolic expressions of church in and through all spheres of the created order, and for the understanding that they are as legitimate an expression of church as local geographical ones. While this may help us to understand that missionary societies and so-called para-church organisa-tions are really expressions of non-local church, this is not all that we are saying here. Rather we envisage that relational groupings will form for whole cities, regions and nations which will facilitate the development of new shapes of church and the reformation of some old ones and that while these need to behave responsibly they have as much validity as local structures of church. The five-fold ministries will often develop more rapidly within these apostolic forms of church and provide the vision and gifting that the more traditional and local expressions of church need in order to re-position themselves into the city and territory in which they are located. It will be necessary for local-church-developed five-fold ministries to welcome the help of this new breed of ministries, as well as being themselves encouraged and released to initiate them. One ideal situation will be where local church leaders have developed to become elders in the town or city. As they look outwards in their responsibility to invade every sphere of life with the gospel they will see the need to develop new shapes and expressions of church. They will realise the need to express church together outside their own local congregations in apostolic ways that release, train and empower people to form these shapes. In some cases it will be the formation of church among unchurched children or youth. In other circumstances it will be the need to find a shape of church appropriate for the business world. Where help is needed from outside the city they will welcome them in. This is happening right now in some English towns and cities like Leeds and Burton-on-Trent that will provide important case studies for the way ahead.

## Elders in Every City

We referred earlier to the story of the Brazilian Church hearing from God about His desire to revive the Church in Europe, in order for us to run together to the ends of the earth. We thank God for the very rich contribution that many Brazilian brothers and sisters are making sacrificially today, both here in Britain and in many other Europeans nations. We know of many who have sold their homes or possessions to finance their coming to these lands and who now are finally being received in many cities. We acknowledge their courage! In particular we are referring to the prophetic word that brought the first wave to Britain. Men and women like Paulo and Lana Borges, Marcos and Nanetta

Barros, Flavio and Karen Guerrata, who handed over the leadership of their local congregations, and moved lock, stock and with many children to our cold and unwelcoming shores with such a biblical word to bring to us, as Paul gave Titus to bring to the Cretans! They said that we should *'set in order what remains, and appoint elders in every city as I directed you'* (Titus 1:5). Now, if we were going to a new nation, we doubt we would have the boldness to bring a word that connotes that the people there are *'... always liars, evil beasts, lazy gluttons ... For this cause reprove them severely that they may be sound in the faith ... They profess to know God, but by their deeds they deny Him, being detestable and disobedient, and worthless for any good deed'* (Titus 1:12–13, 16). To be fair, our Brazilian friends never expressed anything other than deep respect and gratitude for the fact that the gospel had come to them from our forefathers and they wanted to come and say thank you! But to those of us already exercised about the shame of our nations, that they quoted Titus at all seemed rightly to call us to repentance again, and that God really was committed to reproving and disciplining us, as a Father disciplines those whom He loves. It was that which many of us heard first, and only then came the significance of the verse that they brought us. We should set things in order, the things of the grace of God that remain with us to this day, and this will require some careful adjustment. And we should appoint elders in cities.

Now many of us know that, in the time of the New Testament writings, the Church was small enough for only one group to be functioning in one 'city' or town at the time, so when Paul writes to 'the saints' in such and such city, he is writing to all the Christians gathered in one expression of what we would call 'local church' in that place. Or was he? Certainly by the time he was writing to the saints in Rome, there was definitely more than one gathering of them, scattered throughout a major metropolis, but he chose to call them all as one, by the name of their city. Relationships would have been cordial enough to pass the letter round, and with it being somewhat of a laborious task to write and send, it was obviously good stewardship to write the one letter and all share it. After all, it was 'apostles' doctrine' and so the common property of all. So the title of the Christians linked to the place of their living was just pragmatic. Or, again, was it? By the time the Titus reference was brought to our attention, it had a confirming weight to it, as many of us had been considering the issue of territory, and how the Church, in how-ever many of her forms, should be relating to where she was living. Particularly in Britain, many congregations of believers had formed important relationships with other congregations, usually determined by the fact that they held the same doctrines, ecclesiology or practice. The older, more traditional churches had always related in denomina-tions, and now newer forms were also linking up in streams or 'tribes'. There is great strength and purpose in such relationships and indeed we see the tendency for this to happen more and more now catching on in other European nations as well as in North America and throughout the third day Church. But the Holy Spirit is now emphasising the new basis of relating across the body of Christ in relationship to territory.

But 'elders in every city'? Immediately the questions of what kind of authority this would represent were posed. How would one elect such a body, or who would appoint them? What would the qualifications be to function in such a role? Since the everyday use of the term 'elder' had only ever been used to date by Christians in relationship to local congrega-tions, it seemed likely that city elders might be constituted as a board of various church elders, mapping out the city and carving it up into a modern equivalent of parishes, so we might not tread on one another's toes, or steal one another's sheep! Except that both the Catholic and Anglican Churches in Britain had already done this, so a new map would already be a parallel structure. Who would the real elders be? But it was a biblical mandate that Paul was instructing Titus in. We can't even plead it as apostolic behaviour only related to the original twelve in such a case. We had to reconsider that the biblical 'order' that the Church should be set in had to do with functioning together in relationship to common territory.

An Old Testament overview threw some light on the development of the role of an elder. Originally an elder was a person of more mature years who was expected therefore to have gained a measure of wisdom. Perhaps more significantly and challenging for a European would be that they would have been expected to carry something of the corporate history and memory of their people, as tradition, 'the tradition of the elders', was passed down in such a way, told in story form from one generation to another, rooting and grounding the rising generations in their corporate identity. However, the context of the role changes. The term elder was used in the context of a house or household, of a tribe, or even of the whole people of Israel as they wandered through the wilderness when a core of seventy of the elders became Moses' team leadership. But the term and role had been in use by other communities before the Israelites. Genesis 50:7 refers to the elders of Egypt. The cities in the lands they passed through in the exodus had elders with whom they negotiated passage, and by the time the people of Israel had themselves settled in the Promised Land, they also structured themselves around city elders. Jephthah speaks with the elders of Gilead, Boaz with the city elders concerning his marriage to Ruth, and in Ezra there is a council of 'the elders and judges of every city' called together to turn away the anger of God from the whole people.

By New Testament times this role had become synonymous with the Sanhedrin, but as the Spirit of God moved in Jerusalem and a new community of God's people were born and began to move and group and flow into the cities and towns of the regions, in these places, elders were again appointed. They were appointed in the churches (Acts 14:23), but they functioned in relation to the city, as indeed the Church itself was formed to do. The very concept of an elder is community orientated.

## Who, What and Why?

As such today, we suggest that city elders should function at the interface of the Church to the city, to represent the corporality of the Church as smaller more sphere-specific church expressions multiply. They should also therefore, at this corporate level, reflect the structure and complexity of the city as well as the primary functions of Kingdom expression. An eldership in the city that is only constituted of pastors of local congregations would be highly unbalanced. We will expect key Christian businessmen or women, mature Christian teachers, child care officers and musicians or artists to be gifted and called into such a role, as well as younger students or apprentices who are fiery radicals! And their task and practice? To speak the apostles' teaching into the councils and governments of the city, with grace and humour but with bold fearlessness. If God created all things through His word, there must be a body who can speak into the communities of creation. They will fulfil the need to speak out the values of the Kingdom and call the authorities of creation to remember their mandate to promote the good and be a terror to evil. To be effective, they too will need to pursue fellowship with those in authority, to bless them and know them well enough to pray intelligently and lovingly for them. This is true eldership in the gates!

Interestingly, as eldership starts to be recognised functionally in some of the cities we know, the people involved have been through a major learning curve. New skills are needed for leaders to fellowship with their peers. So often Christian leaders have been in a relationship with the church whereby they have friends and relationships, but they are usually built on a paternal model. Indeed, in some training establishments particularly in the more traditional churches, leaders are warned against getting too close or vulnerable with those whom they lead because it will undermine their role and authority. This has left many dangerously exposed to isolation, depression and temptation. Now God is calling for heart relationship, many are willing and indeed hungry for closer friendships, but often don't know whom to turn to. More significantly, in circumstances where they are led by the Holy Spirit to covenant with other men and women in their city for the land, and they meet other carriers of the Kingdom of God, different from them although motivated alike, they are discovering that they lack the skills, even the culture to express these new relationships. It was highly revealing to us when our newly arrived Brazilian friends and helpers made the following observation. They asked the question why most of our churches advertise their Sunday morning activity as a service. Services are for servants. Gatherings, meals, celebrations are for friends. Our expectations of fellowship have been formed by tasks and religious history. Some of us come from very vocal expressive backgrounds and want to talk through how we feel, react, process. Others are more contemplative, sensitive and need more time and space. What will be the dominant culture of building new cross-cultural relationships? Is one way more biblical than another? The very process of discovering the best culture is the most useful, stretching and demanding experience of fellowship. Jesus led His apostolic band through many cultures as they grew together and into the spheres of creation. He began by revealing the Father, then drew them out of servanthood into friendship, and from there became the firstborn of His brothers! Being drawn into new forms of relationship is marvellous discipleship and formidable patterning for the whole body!

City elders must relate around the breaking of bread. As we mentioned earlier this is powerful spiritual warfare and is the one place where the body of Christ can be healed of its divisions; we being many are one body. They will be required to work through the difficulties and insecurities, as mature and representative of the whole. As they stand on behalf of all the different shapes and sizes of church expression in the territory and they stand together, they can powerfully demonstrate and incarnate the unity of the Spirit in the bond of peace. This we believe creates a powerful place in the Holy Spirit which will empower and strengthen all the

Christians in the same territory to receive more grace to experience unity at every level. It is this example and incarnation which creates what many might call a 'covering' for other expressions of church in the city. It is not structural or institutional. It is only as powerful as the love that the unity expresses, but it does facilitate the corporate experience across the territory that it represents.

Then the fully developed role of a city elder will be worked out in all that the broken bread stands for, in their priesthood for and on behalf of the city. As they stand at the interface of the Church with the community, they also stand on behalf of the city in which they too live and work and have their being, and to which they are covenanted, at the interface with heaven. Here they have jurisdiction to stand in the gap for the sins of the city and like Daniel and Nehemiah can repent for and renounce the historical root sins and iniquities which have grieved away the presence and glory of God from the territory. Without unity and covenantal authority, this process by intercessors will only bring a temporary relief. With such a body functioning and 'standing in the land', the ground of healing can be held and the release becomes permanent. What a role and calling!

And so these men and women will be people of prayer! They will lead by prayer and prayer only. Without structural authority, they will have no rights of hire and fire. They will only have prayer! They will pray for one another, and for the body, for the city and for the nation. But at the interface of the land and the heavenly places there is also warfare. Let's call forth strong elder grace in our cities, in order to invade the heavenly places above our land and keep and create an open heaven there. Those who discourage the Church from going boldly forward into spiritual warfare are like Peter who immediately after the Lord had described this aspect of Church said, 'God forbid it, Lord!' and the Lord's reply is the same. This battle aspect of the Church's ministry of the Kingdom of God is clear from four main passages in the gospels, all of which are paralleled in the epistles. Both Matthew and Luke describe the encounter with Satan that the Holy Spirit led Jesus into at the beginning of His ministry and record His direct words of resistance, *'Be gone, Satan!'* (Matthew 4; Luke 4). James and Peter take this up in their epistles with the admonition to *'Resist the devil and he will flee from you'* (James 4:7; cf. 1 Peter 5:9). All three synoptic gospels record Jesus' exhortation to *'bind the strong man'* but Luke uses the word for 'overcome' in the context (cf. Matthew 12:29, Mark 3:27 and Luke 11:21–22). This is the same word that the apostle John takes up to describe the spiritual battle engaged by the seven churches in Revelation (chs. 2, 7, 11, 17 and *passim*). Matthew's account of this essential foundation of Church fits exactly with the climax of Paul's letter to the Ephesians where the mature Church is described in a struggle *'not against flesh and blood, but against the rulers, against the powers, against the world forces of this darkness, against the spiritual forces of wickedness in the heavenly places'* (Ephesians 6:12). Then John records Jesus' perspective of the cross as the power to cast out Satan and confirms it himself in his own epistle with the words,

*'The Son of God appeared for this purpose, that He might destroy the works of the devil.'* (1 John 3:8; cf. John 12:31)

On this basis, they will act decisively.

And they will pray for the nation, since cities link throughout the land itself. City elders cannot be parochial though they must be territorial! They will have a role and responsibility to build spiritual relationships with other cities. In this way the Lord networks the entire land.

There is much that could be added here again about the need to safeguard these new shapes from that old ambitious, self-promoting power hungry desire, promoted by the imperial spirit. Consider it said. Again. And again.

## The Role of the Local Church

As more cells and experimental forms of church spring up across a networked city, what is the new role of what has always been known as 'local church'? It will be threatened by these new developments. Many are in reaction to it and are only too happy to try something new and reject the old. That is not our position. We believe that in the increasing complexity of creation, Church should become as it were a 'mixed economy', but with a very real role remaining for local or what we would call territorial church. Geography is as important as the society it supports, which may change, though the territory probably will not. Therefore local church as we have known it still has a role and some strong foundational principles to incarnate, but it will be more specialised, and there will be some adjustments necessary to ease the inter-relationships with other newly emerging forms of church.

All healthy biblical expressions of church will be structured around the foundational characteristics described by the Lord to the apostles, as we concluded in Chapter 4. We noted that these foundations were the revelation of Christ, the process of discipleship, the war against the strongholds of death and hell, and the release of the Kingdom of God in space and time. The Lord's strategy was to initiate and teach these foundations of Church in its original apostolic expression with a view to them being embodied in specific influential geographical locations. These in turn became examples and centres of the release of the gospel into the surrounding regions, nations and continents. Clearly the Lord planned for Jerusalem to be the first of these centres and the apostles followed His example with Antioch, Ephesus, Corinth, Colossae, Rome and so on. In understanding and evaluating the effectiveness of current forms of local church we obviously need to begin by asking how strongly they are structured around the basic foundations and how securely and deliberately they are rooted into the territory? Since Pentecost it is the work of the Holy Spirit to bring the revelation of Jesus, and the essentials for this are worship and the Word. Local churches must be providers of worship in the Holy Spirit and the ministry of the Word by the power of the Spirit or there will be no ongoing revelation of Christ.

However, for the Holy Spirit to stay in a place He requires unity between the leading disciples in that town or region, because of the territorial nature of this kind of church. Local churches must be in relationship with other territorial churches because they all belong to the one city. This is completely clear from the words of the Lord when He said,

> *'I do not ask in behalf of these alone, but for those also who believe in me through their word; that they may all be one; even as you, Father, are in me, and I in you, that they also may be in us; that the world may believe that you sent me.'*
> (John 17:20–21)

Taken in context these words explain why the Holy Spirit is unable to be present in sufficient power to convince the inhabitants of many of our cities that it is sin not to believe in Jesus (cf. John 16:8–9). There is simply not enough unity between the leaders of His Church in the place. When there is more than one local church expression in a town or region, unity, and where necessary repentance and reconciliation, is absolutely essential for the ongoing revelation of Jesus, whether or not there is good worship and the faithful preaching of the Word.

Secondly, there is the discipleship process. Once again Jesus is our model for doing this. The issue of the nature and structure of leadership and authority is crucial here, and is so important in our European context with the prevalence of the imperialistic spirit that we will revisit it several times more in later chapters. Getting this right is essential to all expressions of Church: apostolic, local, temporary or experimental. At this point it will suffice to point out again that Jesus' discipleship process was from paternity to fraternity, from servants to friends; that humanly speaking His aim was to do Himself out of a job. All our discipleship must be of this type or we will never be examples and centres of the release of the gospel. Instead we will build our own 'ministry' or movement or 'church' organisation and it won't be a true expression of the Church of Jesus Christ or the agent of His Kingdom. Not only did the Lord Himself give His leadership away to the Holy Spirit He never allowed any of His individual followers to take the same position of authority over each other as He had over them in the days of His flesh. Peter was not Jesus' successor but the Holy Spirit was, and when Peter spoke up boldly in his leadership gifting on the day of Pentecost, he stood up with the eleven. While all discipleship begins with an element of paternal authority in it, we must never forget that we are brothers and sisters to those we disciple. This is why Jesus warned us not to be like the Pharisees who

> '... *love the place of honour at banquets, and the chief seats in the synagogues, and respectful greetings in the market places, and being called by men, Rabbi. But do not be called Rabbi; for One is your Teacher and you are all brothers. And do not call anyone on earth your Father; for One is your Father, He who is in heaven. And do not be called leaders; for One is your Leader, that is, Christ. But the greatest among you shall be your servant, and whoever exalts himself shall be humbled; and whoever humbles himself shall be exalted.'*     (Matthew 23:6–12)

Probably one of the most contested essential characteristics of territorial church is our calling to spiritual warfare. This is hardly surprising when you think about it. The devil is seriously against it! This is such an important matter for us in Europe where the Church has been so invaded by demonic powers throughout much of its history. As we have seen, it has never been properly exorcised and so has been seriously hindered in its task of overcoming the gates of hell in our continent. Rather they have overcome us. In the next chapter I (Roger) tell the story of how the Lord insisted that I be in good fellowship with and indeed receive great help from those who disagreed with me about this. Our reason for assessing local church quite critically here is not for the purpose of causing or widening division but to secure the recovery and reformation of the work of the Kingdom of God in Europe. This is of such importance that we had rather risk being misunderstood or disagreed with than fail in the attempt. Our Christological approach to biblical exegesis and theology drives us to the conclusion, as we have already stated, that the Church exists for the purpose of overcoming 'the powers of death' or 'the gates of hell' as it is variously translated. If ever this aspect of the Church's ministry were needed it's right now in Europe. The final chapter of this book will attempt to uncover and explain the strongholds that have overcome us and are standing against us. These are the powers of death that we must overcome at this time. One of the main reasons for establishing local churches is that they become the stronghold of the Kingdom of God in a place. Therefore the concept of a single local congregation setting out to displace the strongholds of the enemy without the united help of other Christians in the city where they exist is unrealistic. But equally, if we together displace the enemy's ancient grip over the land, but fail to establish the stronghold of God in its place, in well established vital worshipping, loving and praying communities, we will not keep the ground. This is the unique and vital role of a territorial, that is local, church.

The final foundation that local church needs to be built upon is the release of the Kingdom of God into the town and region in which it is situated. These keys to the Kingdom operate from the revelation of Jesus on which church is built. As we see and know Him by the Spirit He shows us what the Father is doing. The gifts of the Spirit which He distributes are for doing the Kingdom-bringing work which we see that the Father is initiating. All the motivational gifts that Paul tells us that we have, the supernatural gifts which He tells us to seek, and the gifts that we become, are for this work of bringing the Kingdom of God with power to the locality (cf. Romans 12:6–8; 1 Corinthians 12:8–10; Ephesians 4:11). The use of these gifts mainly or exclusively for in-house church meetings, for the needs of fellow Christians or the development of ministry careers is wrong. Paul makes quite clear that these keys are *'for the equipping of the saints for the work of the ministry.'* The ministry of the Church is the work of bringing the Kingdom of God to those parts of the city which it has not yet penetrated. The particular role of the local church is to relate to geographical territory and build territorial strongholds of the glory of God, but it is also to release and empower every saint among us to function fully as leaders themselves in the spheres where God has planted them. As a leader of a local church, our other main tasks alongside the ministry of the Kingdom into the very territory for which we are responsible is to release and empower those who worship and are discipled among us to function and lead in their spheres of creation. So where there is any tension between our leadership and their responsibility, we must submit to their growth and release. In this season the 'gathered church' must serve the scattered to be faithful.

The implications and consequences of the changing shape of church structure are far reaching and demanding, to say the least. The shapes and possibilities are only just beginning to emerge. There will be a great deal of dying to do, but a whole lot more living as a result. The land must be sown to reap a harvest and while most of the seed is in the storehouse it lies sterile. A body must stand in the land, but while it remains dismembered it is powerless. The Spirit of God is moving again, this time across the face of Europe, whispering of a new day, a resurrection day, and we must rise.

# Chapter 7

# The Fourth Day Dawns!

It is not the first time in history that God has required a people to be ready for paradigmatic change. We are thrilled, though troubled, to be alive at such a time! Many generations have longed to see the glorious impact of God's Kingdom tangibly into their own time and space, and failed to see what we are about to experience. As we look forward, with some realistic trepidation, to this season of change and reorientation, we should pause to strengthen our hearts and minds in God, and humble ourselves again in the light of our corporate history and destiny! Jesus rebuked the people in a season of change because, He said, 'you know how to analyse the appearance of the earth and the sky, but why do you not analyse this present time?' (Matthew 16:2–3). We do need therefore both to position ourselves rightly in the land of our calling, and also to discern the times we are living in. And biblical narrative will help us to do this.

We should be encouraged by the streams of life that invaded our continent over the centuries, with all the strengths and glories with which the different cultural expressions of the gospel have enriched us. We are to be emboldened by the children of the gospel returning to our lands at this point, with their own particular grace and their hearts turned towards us in hope and covenant for a new breakthrough for Europe. We are hearing the cry of the land itself, and the longing of all creation rising for a new revelation of the people of God even from the ashes and the devastations of former generations. For with a backward look, we have also to recognise fully the level of loss and defeat that the Kingdom of God has been allowed to suffer in our nations. Now, if the gospel has reached the uttermost parts of the earth and is rising there, the analogy of the third day when the Lord rose from death is a gloriously apt one, as the revelation of Christ rises in the ends of the earth, even out of the tomb-like experience of the first and second day nations! At this point then we must be prepared to learn from the disciples on the road to Emmaus and be ready for our hearts to burn within us as we consider Him opening our eyes to new perspectives and possibilities that we haven't yet even considered in the Scriptures. What a paradigmatic change was in store for them and is yet for us! It may be that we are presently reacting somewhat like Thomas, hearing what seem to us irrational stories of hope and faith from others, but the level of our disappointment making us unable to grasp for ourselves the full implications unless He appears and allows us to touch His scars. Here is an encouragement to be humbled enough to acknowledge a new need for faith, as *'Blessed are they who did not see, and, yet believed'* (John 20:29). We could resonate with the experience of Peter, knowing the Lord had risen, but still suffering from the as yet unresolved shame and despair of his own failure, needing his heart and affections healed and forgiven but choosing rather to go fishing than face the piercing gaze of Love again. It is of course the Lord who deliberately seeks him out therefore and engages that broken heart, walking along side him on the beach, as a man talks to his friend (John 21).

But we are convinced that as we pan over the development of the gospel in all the earth, we are actually at the dawn of a 'fourth day', and as such the narrative of John 11 is particularly applicable to our time. For the name Lazarus means 'God is helper' and applies so appropriately to Europe as the cradle of the gospel to the Gentiles. Who has God helped as He has helped our nations? Again and again through the centuries, His help has come to us, His presence and His word have enlightened us, enriched our constitutions, developed our welfare systems, birthed our educational establishments and energised our missionary zeal. In all the muddle and mixture of our development, His name and His people have grown up like wheat among tares, as salt that has resisted corruption, as light that has shone into dark corners of our own and others' cultures. But John 11 makes harrowing reading, for when Jesus heard that His friend Lazarus was sick, *'He stayed then two days longer in the place where He was'*, and when He finally came to Judea again, Lazarus *'had already been in the tomb four days'*. During the days of our crisis of faith and identity, our sickness in the old European nations, it seems as though the Lord has preferred to stay away! He's certainly around, and stories of His grace and favour in other nations trickle through to us. But after the captivity of this century, the seemingly total loss of power and even Christian worldview since the 1960s particularly, it does seem that the sickness has taken a toll, even unto death. Yet Lazarus's was the sickness that was not *'unto death, but for the glory of God, that the Son of God may be glorified by it'*! Nevertheless, for this glory to be revealed, the stench of death had to be acknowledged and experienced. There are some depths to be plumbed in this narrative that will help us to live through this exposure of Christian Europe as in some ways stinking, rotten to death, while still known as Jesus' friend whom He loves.

## Raising a Sign to the Nations

Firstly, there is the marvellous overlap of times: Lazarus is going to sign the way, in advance of the full resurrection of the one new man, Jesus. He is going to mark the power and mercy of God that is able to overcome all resistance, even that final great enemy of death. The sign of Lazarus is a forerunner sign that points to an even greater one, when Jesus (and in Him, a new humanity) is resurrected. We believe that in the resurrection of Christian Europe there is a sign and glory that will point to a greater one, the speeding of the gospel into all the earth, including returning to the lands of Israel and the Middle East, from where all revelation of God began in the earth, to a great turning of many in those lands also to Christ, to reconcile *'all things to ... the blood of his cross'* (Colossians 1:20). To the day when one new man will rise up, in whom *'There is neither Jew nor Greek, there is neither slave nor free man, there is neither male nor female...'* (Galatians 3:28), and where the redemption and forgiveness of the sins of Europe will be fulfilled in the restoration of all that was lost through division, disinheritance and murder.

That is why we must take this *kairos* time and word so seriously. Europe and the nations of European peoples are essential to God's plan and glory at this moment for something so much greater than just the restoration of our churches! There is such a wealth of the Lord's revelation deposited in us that needs to be released to show Him glorious in all the earth, both by creation and by redemptive purpose. When I (Sue) first heard the prophetic word about God bringing revival to London, I was honestly affronted! Suffering from an intercessory sense of guilt and shame about our nation and the unrighteousness of our city, my reaction to the prophet was that he hadn't listened closely enough! Now I repent for my arrogance! The Lord gently rebuked me, rather as He did Jonah. If He could win this great city again, what kind of sign would it release in the earth? If God can win proud London, is there anyone or anywhere He **can't** reach? As Paul writes concerning the Gentile nations, we believe that the redemptive purpose of God visiting Europe a second time will be that *'just as* [we] *were ... disobedient to God, but now* [will have] *been shown mercy ... so these also now have been disobedient, in order that because of the mercy shown to you they also may be shown mercy'* (Romans 11:30–31). We are convinced that the power of such a double portion of mercy will provoke other disobedient nations to seek His face. Like Paul we covet that the grace of God shown in the resurrection of European Christianity will so clearly be **only** grace, that it may *'move to jealousy* [Paul's] *fellow countrymen and save* *some of them'* (Romans 11:14). So very much depends on our laying hold of His marvellous initiative!

## A Wholehearted Task

Then there is in this narrative the clear word that in the final crisis of intercession only wholehearted response will break through. Lazarus is going to stand in the gap between life and death, in the same way that Jesus will. He is identifying with Jesus by death as well as by life, and only because of his relationship with the Lord can this be required of him. He is really going to the end of himself and this before ever he has the final great breakthrough of Jesus' own resurrection to undergird his faith. Perhaps Lazarus himself is not even aware of the intercessory role he is playing, but nevertheless his relationship with Jesus places him at the cutting edge of demonstrating the power of the Kingdom of God. But look at that relationship: according to Mary and Martha he shares the name of the apostle John as the one whom Jesus loves. Then the Scripture echoes it, *'Now Jesus loved Martha and her sister and Lazarus'*. It is obvious that Bethany where the three of them lived, was a very special place for Jesus. Though it is Mary who is the demonstrative one pouring out the oil over Jesus' feet, Martha is the busy one who serves noisily and sometimes complainingly, but you know she has a heart of gold and, though nothing else is said about Lazarus, the trio represent the place of family, wholeness, relationship and love. Bethany means 'house of dates': it's a fruitful place, an oasis of heart rest in the midst of working the works of God while it's day. This trio represent *'faith working through love'* (Galatians 5:6). These are the ones who can be trusted with this level of intercessory burden and breakthrough. It is a heart commitment that costs everything but wins fully.

They can function at this level because they know the Jesus who invests His own heart and emotional depths. There is the great sign as Jesus 'troubles Himself' in the face of such death and loss! In the face of His friends' weeping and despair and in the face of death itself, the Scriptures tell us how He groans from His guts or 'snorts like a horse' and then weeps. We must consider again the emotional/spiritual involvement of God Himself in our pain and loss. It is another pointer of something new we have to see and experience, that this battle requires what the New Testament Greek calls *splanskna*, and what the King James Bible often translates as 'bowels of mercies'. Modern English translations usually render it 'compassion'. This is what Jesus was moved by when He encountered the widow of Nain's dead son (cf. Luke 7:13). This is the moving of God's people to their roots, to the guts and not just the intellectual affirmation of doctrine. This is why some of the lessons are coming to us afresh from those lands and cultures where the people function as much out of their hearts as their heads and which we need God's help to receive fully, where head and heart responses can also be reconciled. It is high on God's agenda for us as European peoples to reach out beyond the Graeco-Roman formulae that we are so used to and comfortable in. Our southern brothers and sisters are passionate, but they with those of us from the cooler, more northern nations may still need the healing word of God, like Peter, into our spiritual roots before we can risk our all, head and heart, for the healing of our land.

## The Now of God

It's time for active, passionate, effective faith to be resurrected in Europe. Like Martha and even Mary, many of us would say that we believe that if God had been here during our period of captivity, such death and loss would not have happened. If He had come more powerfully, we might not have yielded so totally to the pride and arrogance of humanistic competition. There is more than a hint of blame that we have come to such a pass, and that it's not ours but God's fault, and reveals a decadent, passive theology! Nevertheless, with a little religious humility, we do still believe that He is God, *'the Christ, the Son of God, even He who comes into the world'* (John 11:27). If He wasn't here when we got into such a mess, maybe He will still come again at some future date and in some future, even rapturous, way to deliver us spiritually. But Jesus stands majestically between what was, or even might have been, and a future somewhat fuzzy, mystical hope, and with His great declaration calls us all to a new now!

> *'I am the resurrection and the life; he who believes in Me shall live even if he dies.* (John 11:25)

Europe can and must come out of her (deserved) tomb! Europe can and must be the sign of the resurrection power of the gospel! Europe can and must be unwrapped of her grave clothes that will otherwise hold us back into our old death experience and hinder us from walking again in a new life and freedom! And we must believe and act so it can happen now!

## Four-fold Ministry

If the fourth day is dawning in the progress of God's Kingdom in the earth geographically, the development of the style of ministry is also changing from the third to the fourth season here in Europe, a new expression for a new day. We wrote earlier of the time of transition we find ourselves in. We used the expression that the Church is moving from a pastor/teacher shape into a prophetic/apostolic posture. Peter Wagner describes it as a time of 'apostolic reformation'. We believe we must understand the times in order to function in the most effective way and that we can track something of the significant changes of times and seasons from the pattern of Jesus' own ministry.

### Good news for the poor

In Luke's Gospel, immediately after His fasting and warfare in the wilderness, Jesus came out into the public arena and announced His purpose:

> *'The Spirit of the Lord is upon Me,*
> *Because He anointed Me to preach the gospel to the poor.*
> *He has sent Me to proclaim release to the captives,*
> *And recovery of sight to the blind,*
> *To set free those who are downtrodden,*
> *To proclaim the favourable year of the Lord.'*
>
> (Luke 4:18–19)

Now this declaration seems to function something like chapter headings for the book of His life that follows. His first activity was to provoke the comfortable religious leaders and demonstrate that good news had come for others! He deliberately refers to God's grace to the widow of Zaraphath and Naaman the Syrian in the Old Testament, those who should have had no access to it under the Law. In Capernaum He reveals the demons in the synagogue and healing for those outside in the streets! He is available with comfort, power and life for lepers, tax collectors and sinful paralytics. He defines and demonstrates both 'good news' and then 'the poor' as those with no way of accessing the revelation of God into the land via the religious authorities. But Jesus sows the good news, the good seed into good ground. He 'evangelises'.

### Release to the captives

So of course the crowds come to Him. And a second phase of ministry kicks in, because they have such need. So like the good shepherd He is, Jesus begins to pastor the huge flock.

> *'...a great multitude of people ... who had come to hear Him and to be healed of their diseases, and those who were troubled with unclean spirits were being cured ... for power was coming from Him and healing them all. And ... He began to say...'*                    (Luke 6:17–20)

This is a very significant time when the poor, having heard good news, are gathered to Him and start to experience a new freedom. The Sermon on the Plain, as it is called in Luke's Gospel, is a time when people are taught new ways of thinking about themselves and the God who loves them (Luke 6:20ff.). The Kingdom of God is for them! The values of the Kingdom are totally different from the values of this world. The rich have their reward now, but God's heart is for the hungry, those who know the emptiness of worldly values and are therefore ready for true riches. He meets their physical, spiritual and personal needs. He pastors them. He *'binds up the brokenhearted'* as it says in the parallel passage in Isaiah 61. And He teaches them. Teaching heals the deepest wounds as it releases them from the captivity of a deceptive and demonic value system. It *'releases the captives'*. We love the impact of the good news of God on those who have never heard about His love and help before. But the impact of the pastor/teacher gift that releases the powerless into a sense of value and destiny and empowers them to challenge injustice and resist evil is a critical form of discipleship.

### Sight to the blind

*'When he had completed all his discourse in the hearing of the people'*, Jesus moved to another posture. Imagine the impact of this change on all those gathered to Him at these times. They have just found such hope, such help and such value. The disciples themselves were Jews and free men, but had been nobody special in the religious world. But now suddenly they were walking and talking with God Himself! A new Kingdom of love and power is here, now, and they are in the middle of it! Settling the crowds down, walking between the groups, handing out supernaturally multiplying picnics, the joy and the wonder must have been beyond belief. The people themselves have all their needs met. This is the fulfilment of all their hopes, joys and dreams. He is the Messiah and He has chosen to share the Kingdom with them. Until a Roman centurion has the cheek to send elders to crash the party. And Jesus is willing to bother about his slave, and to encourage this Gentile oppressor. How far will He go? To share this same value, this same attention with a widow, and even with a dead man. No wonder that *'fear gripped them all, and they began ... saying, "A great prophet has arisen among*

*us!"'* (Luke 7:16). Because just when they thought they were being shepherded, gathered, protected and specially honoured, Jesus reminds them and us that He came to *'open the eyes of the blind'*. He prophesies things that were outside of their paradigm. He has other sheep that are not yet of this fold. He has the walls of fallen expectation to break. He always has desires and purposes that we have never dreamed of, and which, to be honest, may well threaten our own sense of well-being and role. It is a very disturbing season. Fear is normal at such a time. Even John the Baptist starts to question his previous revelation but is encouraged not to be stumbled by the unexpected.

### Sent away

So the fourth season dawns when Jesus calls His disciples to *'"go over to the other side of the lake." And they launched out'* (Luke 8:22). After the stretching signs of how big this Kingdom is going to reach (to Gentiles, slaves, women and even the dead!), it must have been a little reassuring for the disciples to be asked to get in their boat and take to the lake! But even in their comfort zone, the impact of this transition overwhelms them. For they are going to the country of the Gerasenes which is *'opposite to Galilee'*. It doesn't come more different than this. It's a Gentile area, a garrison town for the Romans, and Legion is a sign. Even before they reach the shore, they are overcome by the storm, as here in the strong grip of the enemy, the creation itself rises against them. Jesus, of course, is completely at rest, trusting them to trust Him. The point is this. When Legion is so wonderfully delivered and saved, he begs to come and follow Jesus. He expects to do what all the other crowds, disciples and saved have done until now, but Jesus *'sent him away'*. Why? Because the Spirit of the Lord was on Jesus, to *'apostle away free those who were crushed.'* From this time on, even after the return to Galilee, His disciples are gathered irregularly, but they are sent out, apostled, to go into the towns and villages where Jesus would come after them now, instead of them after Him. The seventy are likewise sent out two by two. The final thrust of Jesus' ministry is that those He has won, discipled and destabilised are now launched out. Everything has changed.

It has changed for us too in Europe at this time. We have had such a long season when the Lord has extended the time for us to be gathered together, to be taught, healed up. Following on from the evangelistic strength of the moves of God in revival at the beginning of the last century, the gift of pastor/teacher was, until the renewal movements of the 1960s and 1970s, largely expressed by one man in a congregation. Through the renewal, the process of Ephesians 4 began to be fulfilled which says that the purpose of a gift in the church is to equip the saints for the work of ministry. The creation of small groups, housegroups or cell groups in most local congregations, whatever their denomination or ecclesiology, is testimony to the fact that now most church members are equipped to pastor one another or share wisdom from the Scriptures together. But this has also given us role and value, and the disconcerting whispers that this might not be the final shape or purpose of our church experience are most provoking. Prophetic words, experiences and even signs can seem destabilising and somewhat unhelpful. But the Lord is moving on. It's time for the apostolic gift to be imparted to the whole body. It is time to turn the Church inside out and send her out into new and uncharted territory. The fourth day is dawning.

## Four Generations

Let's look at it from yet another perspective, in case there remains any doubt about developmental, 'times-sensitive' activity! We also referred earlier to the way in which God builds up to a *kairos* moment of opportunity, through the overlap of three generations: *'I am the God of Abraham, Isaac and Jacob'*. Now much has been said and written about the different contributions that the different generations play in envisioning, consolidating and establishing God's work in a land. Interestingly, in the stories of Abraham and his children, these contributions are marked by what they build, and all three of them create four symbols. Abraham builds four altars. He is the seeker, the visionary, who breaks open points of reconnection with the God who is seeking him. Each altar takes him to a new and clearer revelation of who God is. Isaac digs four wells. In the same land that his father obediently entered, connecting it to heaven, he had dug wells but they had been filled in. Now his son re-digs them and, through conflict and struggle, he arrives through to a consolidated place where the water, the image of God's presence, is flowing consistently and sufficiently to sustain settlement (see Genesis 26). It's a pastoral season and the people gather to the wells. But Jacob is a restless son, with desires and visions for that which was not his expected inheritance! He's reaching out for something else, something more. It's a disturbing, prophetic season. He goes back and forth through the whole land and builds four pillars. Jacob has to address certain issues, notably in his own nature and history ready for a new future. The pillars, anointed with oil, become points of reconciliation or resolution: between heaven and earth at Bethel, between past generational patterns of unrighteousness (Laban) and future generations at Mizpah, between his life in the flesh (Jacob) and his life in the Spirit (Israel) when God spoke again to him at Bethel, and between death and disillusion (Rachel dying in childbirth with Be-oni) and God's promised inheritance (Benjamin) (see Genesis 27–35).

And all this to bring in new authority to the land. Twelve sons (the number for government) are born who will become twelve patriarchs, establish twelve tribes, twelve gates in the foundations of the future city of God. Three generations who are faithful to God, each in their time, will create such a window of opportunity, such a foundation, such a stronghold for God that blessing will follow through countless generations!

So what of the role and responsibility of the next, the fourth generation? God uses and establishes them all as we know with hindsight through their children and their children's children. Wonderfully and climactically, Jesus is born of

Judah. But immediately following on from such a marvellous breakthrough being established, most of them were not much to write home about! The hard work had all been done, so what was left was for them to enjoy the fruit of it and make sure no one disturbed the inevitable and eventual outworking of it all. But there was one, the son of the beloved, who insisted on dreaming. Like his great-grandfather Abraham, Joseph is the one who is going to dream dreams and see visions (his story is of four sets of dreams). Like his grandfather Isaac, Joseph is a *'fruitful bough by a spring'* (Genesis 49:22), who is going to continue to draw from the wells of God's life for himself. Like his father Jacob, his *'branches run over a wall'* (49:22) and he will invade areas hitherto unknown to him or his people! Joseph is going to invade nations and *'push the peoples, all at once, to the ends of the earth'* (Deuteronomy 33:17). Joseph is the sign of God's Kingdom being carried into, serving and ruling in a pagan land. Joseph is the sign of the apostolic season as he is 'sent away' by his brothers but truly by God, as he suffers rejection and injustice but submits to the discipline of God in and through it all. Joseph is the sign and the challenge of our times.

Four is the number of creation. The Trinity was and then formed the creation, the fourth element. In the unseen but revealed realm of John's vision, the four living creatures represent creation in worship around the throne of God. In this, the dawn of the fourth day of God, it is the whole of creation that is calling us to engage, as the carriers of the Kingdom of heaven, in and through all spheres that God has created. And particularly into the cities that have come to be expressions of 'concentrated creation' and which God Himself has redemptively chosen, even to marry!

## Four-square Temple

In order to discover the way ahead for the Church and the work of the Kingdom in Europe in this time of transition, we not only need to analyse the foundational definitions of where we have come from, but to understand the shape of Church and city that we are heading to. This future vision is wonderfully provided in Scripture in the form of the four-square temple of Ezekiel's vision, and the four-square city of the apostle John's Revelation (cf. Ezekiel 40–47 and Revelation 21–22).

In Ezekiel's vision the new temple provides for the return of the glory of God to His people. The four-square temple is the sign of God dwelling in the midst in His temple in the midst of His world. The temple is at the centre of a renewed city and nation. It is where a holy priesthood maintains the purity of the worship and the service of the sacrifices, the government is held accountable, and justice is accomplished for the poor. But this four-square perfect temple does not exist for itself. For out from the altar, out under the eastern gate, inland towards the neighbouring nations, runs the river of God. It's a huge river, approximately a mile to the middle. The river flows to the Arabah, the desert nearest to the cursed lands of Edom. From there it goes to the Dead Sea, which again speaks of the judgement and curse that lies over those lands. Wherever the river goes, everything comes alive. The dead waters become fresh and they are teeming with fish. Fishermen line the coasts of the sea. On both sides of the river all the way to the sea are all kinds of trees full of fruit and the leaves of the trees are for healing. The healed land is to be allotted to the tribes of Israel but with the very clear condition that all the aliens in their midst and their descendants will be included as if native born. Note that the direction is out from and away from the temple. It is towards the alien lands and aliens are included in the inheritance.

If we apply a Christological hermeneutic in good biblical fashion we see that Jesus is the dwelling place of God, the fulfilment of the sacrifice and the place where the glory of God dwells. He said,

> *'"Destroy this temple, and in three days I will raise it up."*
> *The Jews therefore said, "It took forty-six years to build this*
> *temple, and will you raise it up in three days?" But He was*
> *speaking of the temple of His body.'*          (John 2:19–20)

Furthermore, the glory with which He was filled was the glory which we have already seen to be the eternal life, the revelation of the knowledge of God that is the defining possession of every true believer and the foundational building block of Church. (See the beginning of Chapter 4.) As Jesus tells the Father,

> *'...the glory which You gave Me I have given to them, that they may be one just as We are one.'* (John 17:22 NKJV)

Then He sends them to extend this temple, this dwelling place of glory, *'As the Father has sent Me, I also send you'* (John 20:21) and *'Go therefore and make disciples of all the nations'* (Matthew 28:19). Paul describes the work of the cross as bringing together the tribes of Israel with the tribes of the Gentiles. He says of us all,

> *'So then you are no longer strangers and aliens, but you are fellow heirs with the saints, and are of God's household, having been built upon the foundation of the apostles and prophets, Christ Jesus Himself being the corner stone, in whom the whole building, being fitted together is growing into a holy temple in the Lord...'* (Ephesians 2:19–21)

Hence the fulfilment of Israel's inheritance, seen in Ezekiel's vision of the four-square temple, points forward to the fulfilment of the inheritance of all the nations and it reaches them through the river that flows from the Church, the body of Christ, out to the cities, nations and continents of the earth.

But what has so often happened is that the flow has been reversed and the Church has become the means of dominating and ruling over people. Instead of holding governments accountable for justice, instead of working for the inheritance of all the tribes of the earth, we have been invaded by spirits that have caused us to work to legitimate and empower only our own nation or empire. Even when the Church has got free from state domination the same spirits have shaped us so that our structures and leadership gifts work only or mainly for the good of our own members. Breaking free from this is easier said than done, but it has to be done if we are to learn the lessons of European church history and find today's redemptive purpose. There is much more to be said about this both theologically and practically. But before we go any further, we want you to hear Roger's testimony of how God began to turn him around in his own experience as an apostolic leader.

## Ignorance

We have already written about our understanding and experience of the outpourings of the Spirit from the 1990s onwards. We have no doubt that these are part of the contemporary manifestation of the river of God and His plans for our continent. My own struggles with and break-through into more of this fullness fits Ezekiel's own experience as the man with the measuring line led him into the river. My spiritual history began in the Brethren move-ment. Although rooted in revival and part of the Nonconformist response to state Christianity, it had formed itself into an exclusive expression of Church. While some-times eager to grow and evangelise and indeed playing an important part in the final stages of the European mission, the shape and direction was geared to withdrawal from the world. Despite its separation from state Christianity, it was now in great danger of creating a little empire for itself under the guise of exclusive spiritual correctness. The Church was a separated body existing as an alternative society, not an invasive force releasing the Kingdom of God into the nation. As a result I was largely ignorant both of the gospel of the Kingdom and the empowerment of the Holy Spirit that went with it. But I was young, and aware of something missing. So when I encountered Charismatic renewal back in the 1960s and then found fellow Christians who were rediscovering the gospel of the Kingdom I threw myself into inner-city church planting with as much of the Holy Spirit as I was ready for. I was up to my ankles in the river and, frankly, that's where I stayed for the next twenty-seven years. By the early 1990s our relative success in church planting compared with the increasing decline in the condition of London convinced me that something was seriously wrong. I was not ungrateful to God or my colleagues for what we had achieved together. But I was not serving the Kingdom of God in London fully enough. Something else needed to happen.

## Pride

In 1993 two important things happened to me in the space of two weeks. The first was the conference of the Spiritual Warfare Network called Gideon's Army. It took place in Seoul, Korea on an extraordinary prayer mountain belonging to the Kwang Lim Methodist Church. (I write about this in detail in the book *Sins of the Fathers* (Sovereign World, 1999) written with Brian Mills.) Here, in company with leaders and intercessors from around the world, I discovered the power of the cross to forgive the sins of nations, and the role of the Church to overcome the powers of death and hell by standing in the gap on behalf of their nation. It began with Dr Paul Ariga from Japan confessing the sins that the Japanese had committed against the Korean people during the Japanese occupation of Korea. It was as if the Holy Spirit highjacked the conference and from then on every one was repenting for their nation's sins, except the Europeans! Somehow every sin confessed seemed to be connected to us British in some way. In the end we got together with our fellow Europeans and asked them to pray for us as we were the cause of the embarrassment, and with their support somehow we began the painful process of identificational repentance towards the many nations present whom we had sinned against historically. I had little or no theology then for what we were doing, only the prompting of the Holy Spirit in so many hearts. The following week I was visiting Ed Silvoso's Prayer Evangelism conference in the context of the Argentine revival. As the plane landed I heard the Lord telling me to repent to the Argentine Christians for the Falkland War before I said anything else, so I did. It was an extremely radical thing to do in those days, and at that time I would have been the only person they had heard attempt such an apology. It was so humbling that it broke something in me that had grown up over the years – an inner resistance to receiving help or prayer from strangers or people whose spiritual pedigree I was unsure of. I explained it to myself in terms of keeping myself spiritually pure, but really it was pride. So to my knowledge I'd never rested in the Spirit before then. But in the Olmos prison, in the heart of the Argentine revival, converted murderers, rapists and drug dealers prayed for me over and over again, picking me up from the floor and sending me down again until I was so drunk I couldn't walk. At last I was up to my knees in the river.

## Control

I returned to London convinced that God wanted His people to reach it together, whatever their tribe or denomination. Determined to convince leaders that now was the time to give God His Church back I tried everything I knew how to bring leaders together, but with only limited success. Something more had to change in me. Then in June 1994 while a bunch of like-minded leaders from across the nation were meeting in London to pray (part of the Building Together network previously mentioned), the Holy Spirit dramatically visited us. As with many other groups at that time, the visitations continued frequently, pretty much on a daily basis. The following weekend I was helping lead a church leadership conference. Up until then I'd never realised with what tight control I exercised my leadership gifts. I saw it as pastoral concern and responsibility. It was really the fear of man and the need to protect my leadership position. In one of the meetings the Holy Spirit began to manifest all over the room. I was convinced that I had to take control, just to say something sensible to allay people's fears. I resolved in my mind what it should be: 'There's nobody here that wants anything but to do God's will and please Him.' I would say something like that. But it seemed to be taking so long to get the words out. After what seemed an age of stuttering and stammering, I resolved to take a run at it. 'There's nobody here,' I shouted, and fell off the platform into the congregation. My strong control of the Holy Spirit was broken and I was up to my loins in the river. Nearly out of my depth but not quite. The last quarter of a mile was still to come.

## Identity

I did not have long to wait. A few days later Rodney Howard Browne, the South African revivalist, was due to visit Birmingham. If it's not obvious to you yet, I'm seriously into spiritual warfare. As I have said, I believe it to be one of the defining characteristics of Church. I soon discovered that Rodney did not agree with my theology. He had no idea that I was there or who I was, of course. But it became rapidly obvious to me that if everyone believed him, and he was quite persuasive, then no one would read my books, listen to my tapes or come to my seminars! My work might be seriously called into question. Then came the quiet voice of God to disturb me forever. Would I receive more of the Holy Spirit from this man? Would I place the will of God and revival in Europe over and above my position, my right to be right, my identity in ministry, church, or movement? The issue wasn't about whether I was right or he was. It was a matter of what the gospel, church and ministry are for. Would I forever move out from building my ministry, our church, our movement and cast off into the river of the Spirit, out of my depth and into God's? It was no contest and my decision to go for it was accompanied by the craziest manifestation that I've yet encountered. Into my head came some words of Smith Wigglesworth that I'd never understood before. He once said that he was a thousand times bigger on the inside than on the outside. It sounded proud, yet I knew he was not proud. Then I was aware of growing tall so rapidly that I felt I would have to get out of the building before I hit my head on the roof! (It was actually a large high-roofed warehouse.) Before I fully realised what I was doing, I stood up and set out across the rows in front of me, as if I had the legs of a giant, heading for the gangway. The last thing I remember properly until some time later was falling down headlong in the gangway with the thought 'I'll hit my head on the platform' which was all of fifty feet away. The problem with so many of us leaders is that we too are subtly shaped by the spirits of empire, building our temple not God's, or worse, trying to occupy His temple for our kingdom. This has to break, and when it does the size of our gifts and lives together is massively greater than the sum of the parts.

## Four-square City

And we need this to happen because we are heading together for an expression of the Kingdom of God bigger than anything we have yet experienced. It is this that we have to prepare the ground for in the towns and cities of this continent. This is the Four-square City in John's vision. As a city it defies imagination. It's a cube one hundred and fifty miles high. Bear in mind that Mount Everest is only five miles high! Of course we are speaking here in the context of the new heaven and the new earth, so it's difficult to get our minds round how to interpret these kinds of statistics. But for sure it's huge. What we can say is that it's the fulfilment and consummation of our work and calling. While we know that it will ultimately come as the result of the radical interven-tion of God, its coming is what we are aiming for. So we conclude that the shape of it is the shape that we want to bring to our cities. There will come a point, as Jesus said, when *'this gospel of the Kingdom shall be preached in the whole world for a witness to all the nations, and then the end shall come'* (Matthew 24:14). He wants our preaching, in word and action, to be end-shaped!

To see what this will mean it is very illuminating to compare Ezekiel's four-square temple with John's four-square city. The first and most obvious thing to note is that one is a temple and one is a city! We have seen that the Lord likens the Church to the temple and that the river of God flows out from it to the city and to the nations. The river is flowing to this new Jerusalem. This city does not just welcome aliens, but kings and nations are also part of it. The second thing to notice is that the New Jerusalem has no temple in it!

> *'And I saw no temple in it, for the Lord God, the Almighty, and the Lamb, are its temple.'*          (Revelation 21:22)

This is key in at least two ways. It underlines again that the purpose of the Church today is not to create a centre or a temple for the Church in the city or even to devise structures and strategies to get the city to the Church. Rather it is to discover ways of getting the glory of God and of the Lamb to the heart of the city. Then it also explains why the new city of Jerusalem is described in terms which more usually apply to the Church: 'bride', 'tabernacle', 'temple'. This is because the task of the Church is to make the city the dwelling place for God, to infuse the city itself with the shape and DNA of the Kingdom of God, to sow itself into the city, not to have the city serve the Church.

This interplay of the Church and the city, representing the creation of God and, though fallen, the true arena for His glory, is the subject of such confusion historically. How does the glory get via the Church into the world, without the darkness of the polluted creation infecting the Church? This is the ultimate question for this significant moment, as the tide is turning and God is preparing, calling and trusting His Church again to flow like His river or be scattered like His seed into the fullness of the earth. The biblical narratives and all the prophetic signs mark this as such a time. The image of the end of God's plan is that the city should be seen to be glorious and the temple, Church or vehicle which carried the glory there is no longer in sight because they have succeeded! This is the vision of the future that should inform our present. The Church, carrying and flowing in the glorious gospel of the Kingdom, must head full on into the city.

But we must understand the subtle and essential distinction to be made here. We are to serve a city or a nation so that the Kingdom of God and the glory of God and the Lamb are its light! We are not to become subverted and dominated by the spirit powers of a city so that the Church becomes itself the tool and supporter of the darkness in the city. It is understanding this issue and getting the process of moving from the temple to the city right that is the redemptive purpose of the Church in Europe.

# Chapter 8

# Strongholds in the Gates

We are convinced that this is a time of enormous opportunity for Europe, perhaps unprecedented since the days of Constantine. The prayers of the body of Christ in the rest of the earth are fast being mobilised to focus on us for the next five years. Some of the best leadership gifts they have are coming to help us. Those prayers and those gifts are being used by the Holy Spirit to bring about a move of God that will transform our continent if only we are truly willing. As yet we only dimly perceive what needs to be done. But for sure we now have some of the ingredients to make the tracks for the revival train to travel down, and can begin to understand how to avoid the pitfalls that have blocked and derailed the past moves of God. This time we must see the river flow out from the people of God and into the cities and spheres of the Europe of today. We are looking for a massive harvest of souls, and much more. We are looking for the complete transformation of the continent to a level of saturation that fulfils its redemptive purpose and hastens the return of the King. In summary, the prayers that are being targeted on Europe need to be received and acted on in faith by intercessors, apostles and prophets in our nations, cities and regions. Their purpose is to facilitate the process of change in the shape of Church to become an intercessory, prophetic and apostolic people. They will need to pray and work to achieve unity across the body of Christ, until the primary focus of the Church in the city is no longer the local expressions of various denominations and streams. Instead, it will be the transformation of the city with the good news of the Kingdom of God. The tools for this are many. They include informed, strategic intercession that uncovers the wounds and past sins that need confessing and healing, and revelation about the satanic strongholds that need to be overcome. They include prophetic acts of identificational repentance to deal with the sins and wounds, and strategic level spiritual warfare to bind and disarm the powers that inhabit the subsequent strongholds. And they include the mobilisation and empowerment of an army of men and women invading and standing strong in all the streets and spheres of society, with grace and authority to overcome evil with good by their words, works, wonders and lifestyles.

## Strongholds in the Gates

The Lord's messages to the seven churches in John's Revelation provide massive biblical insight into this task. Situated across Asia Minor in what is now modern Turkey, they were the gateway cities into Europe. Each message contains a brief overview of what is going on in the Church in the city, and expresses the challenge and reward of overcoming the obstacles to the gospel of the Kingdom there. Only one of the cities still survives: Smyrna, now Izmir, which at last has a church once again. None of the other churches survived and nor did their cities. It follows that the strongholds the churches faced overcame them. This is highly significant because they were the front line for the gospel that took such hold in Europe. The strongholds that defeated them are the same strongholds that went on to weaken and defeat the Church in Europe throughout the subsequent centuries. If we can understand what they were, and how they could have been overcome, we will have some vital clues for winning the spiritual battle that faces us. We have already noted that seeds of destruction that corrupted the gospel in the European day of world mission have found their way even into some of the expressions of the third day Church. As we examine these churches and their cities we can find redemptive purpose in our past failures, which will point the way to the completed reformation that both we and the third day Church need if we are to complete the work of the Kingdom of God in our generation. Then, as an army of overcomers, we will be ready to recover those modern gateway cities right back to Jerusalem.

## Understanding Strongholds

We are using the word 'stronghold' in a particular way. What we mean by it is an agreement or covenant which is worked out in practice on earth by a group of people and which is affirmed and established in and from the heavenly realm by angels. It is immediately evident that this can be for good or for evil. In the book of Revelation, John is taught to see the churches established in the land and connected to an angel in the heavens. God established this connectivity in creation. God, who is Spirit, drew humankind up from the dust in the seen realm, and walked and talked with them daily. When the angel Satan came to tempt humankind, he clothed himself in reptile form. The Scriptures have always recognised this overlap and interaction of heaven and earth. It is this connection that Jesus came to re-establish.

> *'You have made him a little lower than the angels. You have crowned him with glory and honour and set him over the works of Your hands. You have put all things in subjection under his feet.'* (Hebrews 2:7–8 NRSV)

He came from the highest point of heaven to become *'lower than the angels'* in order to bridge the gap between the heavens and the earth. In fact He went all the way down through the created order to the depths of Hades itself: *'He also had descended into the lower parts of the earth'* (Ephesians 4:9). But from there He went all the way back:

> *'He who descended is Himself also He who ascended far*
> *above all in the heavens, that He might fill all things.'*
>
> (Ephesians 4:10)

On the earth itself, we need similarly to make connections, agreements, between people that fix things. Even God Himself said, *'Let Us make man in Our image'* (Genesis 1:26). He created humankind as corporate because *'even in your law it has been written, that the testimony of two men is true'* (John 8:17). It is in these agreements, in these connections, that strongholds develop and out of them that kingdoms rise and fall.

Satanic strongholds build up from the starting point of individual sin and end in corporate demonisation. A brief case study of Judas Iscariot provides a clear, biblical illustration of this process. John gives us the first concrete evidence of Judas's sin when he complained about Mary's extravagant use of her expensive perfume to anoint the Lord:

> *'Now he said this, not because he was concerned about the*
> *poor, but because he was a thief, and as he had the money*
> *box, he used to pilfer what was put into it.'*     (John 12:6)

At this stage, although his sin was obviously ongoing, he could have got free simply by repenting to the Lord and the other disciples. But continual sin eventually constitutes an invitation to the devil to begin to take control of our heart and mind. So John records that by the pre-Passover supper the devil had *'already put into the heart of Judas Iscariot, the son of Simon, to betray Him'* (John 13:2). By this point Judas would have needed a measure of deliverance to break free. Satan already had free access to his heart. But the next step was the most decisive. Having already washed Judas's feet the Lord extended him the intimate gesture of a morsel of food from the shared pot. The scripture describes how, after he had deceptively accepted the gesture, *'Satan then entered into him'* (John 13:27). Luke tells us that immediately following this Judas *'went away and discussed with the chief priests and officers how he might betray Him to them. And they were glad and agreed to give him money'* (Luke 22:4–5). So we can see how Judas went from stealing, through satanic oppression, to possession and then on to **agree** with the chief priests to form a stronghold of murder against Jesus and His Kingdom. It is through this process of temptation followed by demonisation that Satan typically forms and expands the strongholds of his influence in a city, region or nation.

But how could a follower of Jesus be picked off like this? We suggest that it was because a massive stronghold of the enemy was already in place. This is not to excuse Judas, but it explains the many betrayals or at least denials that have undermined and brought down even genuine apostles in the battle for the Kingdom of God in our time. A process of demonic strategy against Israel over the centuries had led to the rising of a demonised generation. The Old Testament Scriptures close with the recognition of this. They state that unless the hearts of the fathers return to the children and the hearts of the children to the fathers, a curse will come on the land (Malachi 4:5–6). Restored agreement between generations is deeply significant for bringing the former glory to bear on the future, and the power of the ages to come into the present! The lack of reconciliation in this area brought five hundred years of spiritual curse and darkness on Israel. This only began to be turned back with the coming of John the Baptist as a forerunner in the spirit and power of Elijah *'to turn the hearts of the fathers back to the children, and the disobedient to the attitude of the righteous; so as to make ready a people prepared for the Lord'* (Luke 1:17).

In the light of all this it is very informative to look at Jesus' encounter with the Pharisees as described by Matthew (ch. 12). In the story of the exorcism which Jesus tells them, the unclean spirit returned with seven others to re-occupy the 'house' and so the man's state was worse than at first. This time the story is not about one man as it is in Luke's Gospel (cf. Luke 11:26) for Jesus says, *'That is the way it will also be with this evil generation'* (Matthew 12:45). It is about the demonisation of a whole generation. That was why the Lord was so tough with the Pharisees and the other

Jewish leaders of His day, such as when He publicly declared, *'You are of your father the devil, and you want to do the desires of your father'* (John 8:44). The context is Jesus' teaching about the Kingdom of God after John the Baptist had asked for reassurance. He has said that no one born of woman is greater than John but that while he, John, was the messenger that prepared the way, there is now a new Kingdom and the very least in it is greater than John. He then describes a violent spiritual clash of kingdoms:

> *'From the days of John the Baptist until now the kingdom of heaven suffers violence, and violent men take it by force.'*
> (Matthew 11:12)

## Overcoming Strongholds

Then Jesus begins to reproach the **cities** in which He has been working for their failure to repent. He declares that His revealed Kingdom is carrying something so powerful that even the strongholds of the territories of Tyre and Sodom would have fallen to Him. He rejoices over the new solidarity that He and the Father are establishing and to which others are invited:

> *'Come to Me, all who are weary and heavy-laden, and I will give you rest.'*
> (Matthew 11:28)

And so Matthew records how this group or Kingdom stronghold around Jesus walked through the grain fields on the Sabbath day. We now understand this to be the original apostolic travelling band or church. It was this new godly stronghold that encountered the devil's citadel in such power. Yet this satanic power was so embedded in the region that, though it could not prevent His miraculous signs, it resisted His Kingdom just as strongly as the cities of Bethsaida and Chorazin had done (Matthew 11:20–24). This resistance caused Jesus to withdraw from the territory (Matthew 12:15).

This is the kind of stronghold we are up against in Europe today. Not only are whole cities demonised but strongholds have combined together over centuries to demonise a whole generation. The Pharisees were leaders, fathers, in the nation at a crucial time when the multitudes were lost but at last the Kingdom of God was breaking through. The fact that they used biblical truth, the Law, to promote the opposite of the purpose for which it was given, made their position even more inexcusable. It was given to those who were covenanted to the Father for the purpose of blessing all the families of the earth. The Lord knew that this was the opposite of what they were doing. They had turned the Law into a legalistic religious correctness for the purpose of safeguarding their leadership position. Hence His head-on clash:

> *'But if you had known what this means, "I desire compassion not a sacrifice," you would not have condemned the innocent.'*                        (Matthew 12:7)

Hence His deliberate decision to heal on the Sabbath in the incident that followed. This clash of strongholds caused a temporary setback for the Lord. The Pharisees took counsel against Him and He withdrew from the territory. He was not about to risk any physical confrontation with them at this point. His time had not yet come (cf. John 7:6). He had not only come for Israel but for the nations. And He had not come just to win a battle but to restore the lost. As Matthew understood, He had vast prophecies to fulfil.

> *'...He shall proclaim justice to the Gentiles.*
> *He will not quarrel, nor cry out;*
> *Nor will anyone hear His voice in the streets.*
> *A battered reed He will not break off,*
> *And a smouldering wick He will not put out,*
> *Until He leads justice to victory.*
> *And in His name the Gentiles will hope.'*
>                        (Matthew 12:18–21)

The Pharisees had no choice but to surrender or directly oppose Him. As a group they chose the latter. So they accused Him of casting out demons by the prince of demons. Jesus' answer to their accusation is very important for us today:

> '...if I cast out demons by the Spirit of God, then the kingdom of God has come upon you. Or how can anyone enter the strong man's house and carry off his property, unless he first binds the strong man? And then he will plunder his house.'                    (Matthew 12:28–29)

Very revealingly Luke describes the same occasion but uses the word 'overcome' instead of 'bind' with reference to the strong man, which is of course the same word that Jesus used to the seven churches. Clearly, 'bind' and 'overcome' are interchangeable in this context. This is the clue to Jesus' hope and ultimate victory. He withdrew from the territory where the stronghold was located that helped keep a generation in bondage. But only until He had bound the strong man! Then He plundered his house. He did this on the cross when, at the right time, He freely gave Himself up to the power of the chief priests and Pharisees. The fact that Jesus knew that this was happening is clear through His words to Pontius Pilate,

> 'You would have no authority over Me, unless it had been given you from above; for this reason he who delivered Me up to you has the greater sin.'                    (John 19:11)

On the cross He faced right up to this stronghold. As He let it reject and kill Him, He in fact laid hold of it! He bound it to His own death and in His resurrection He triumphed over it.

> 'And having disarmed the powers and authorities, he made a public spectacle of them, triumphing over them by the cross.'
> (Colossians 2:15 NIV)

## Strategies against Strongholds

This is what we must learn to do in the demonised Europe of the twenty-first century. Like the Lord we must strategise to win a city. Resisted by the small provincial towns, He headed inexorably towards Jerusalem. Cities, as we have already seen, are keys to a region and eventually a nation or a continent. We have already referred to Ed Silvoso's now famous account of how the pastors of the city of Resistencia came together in unity and then were able to uncover and overcome the occult power of San La Muerte or Saint Death, which, they discovered, held the city in its power, much like Ephesus under the power of Artemis (recorded in Ed Silvoso's book *That None Should Perish*, Regal Books, 1994). The Church in Resistencia grew by three hundred per cent as a consequence. In the revival contexts of the third day Church there are now many such examples of cities in the process of being transformed in this way. In scores of European cities, invariably with the help and inspiration of our brothers and sisters from the uttermost parts of the earth, this process of transformation is now also beginning to take place. But we need biblical help and revelation for the way forward – help which the risen Christ's messages to the seven churches contain.

Each one of these churches was known by their city and was drawing up the corporate memory of the city and the land in which it was planted. As such there were layers of history held in the land that the Lord wanted to sift. This was for them what it is also today for us: both their best potential and their worst danger. The ancient shape and calling of the land was waiting for them to fulfil and speak out. The prayers and prophecies of those living there before them were waiting for the agreement of today's people of God to bring them to fruition. But so too were the wrong choices, the false covenants and idolatries of the past laid down like maturing wine in the land to which they were called. And they were also fully connected to the heavenlies, carrying their calling and destiny and providing angelic help to strengthen and serve it. But here too were the pressures of spiritual strong-holds warring with the purposes of God. And God knew how much depended on them and us finding the way through all the morass of pressure and confusion, to clarity of calling and destiny. Now He is depending on us. So we must learn much from these instructions!

## Encouragement

The Lord applauds each city church because the Holy Spirit is the Comforter and the Encourager and these men and women were paying the ultimate price to break through. The greatest encouragement lies therefore, in helping them to see the root area that potentially empowers the Enemy against them. The glory of these passages is that the Lord has the pre-emptive strike already planned. He knows how to counter these strongholds by sowing a specific revelation of Christ into the depths of the Church and therefore the city, the wonderful counter-offensive of the cross and resurrection, which good will overwhelm the evil planned! By considering the 'opposite spirit', the antidote to the weakness pointed out, we can discern even more clearly the nature of the temptations which did in fact, first time round, eventually cause these churches to flounder. We believe that by the time the gospel passed through their gates into the European continent, the root sins to which the Lord refers were already at work in these cities. They had built the foundations for the strongholds of the enemy, which ever since have locked us into a measure of the same loss. But in these days of the final thrust of God, as it gathers momentum from the uttermost parts of the earth to surge back into Europe and then on, returning again in power to the land of our fathers and the lands of our creation, the Lord is drawing us back again to His wisdom. If we can grasp the fullness of God's revelation in these seven letters, and if we can obey the lessons they contain, we may yet discover the keys for unlocking our continent and the great final onslaught of the Lord's army into the earth!

# Ephesus

> *'To the angel of the church in Ephesus write, The One who holds the seven stars in His right hand, the One who walks among the seven golden lampstands, says this: "...I have this against you, that you have left your first love."'*
>
> (Revelation 2:1, 4)

As He speaks to the church at Ephesus, the Lord is depicted holding the angelic sphere in His hand and walking among the churches, those destined to be the stronghold of His light and truth. To those who overcome in this trial, the promise and reward related to this issue is to eat of the Tree of Life, the eternal presence of the Lord. The church at Ephesus is called to signify the role of the people of God in re-establishing and inhabiting the right connection between the unseen and the seen realm, between the heavens from which our life comes and the earth from which we were made. We believe that all churches are called to this, and Ephesus is the sign of this calling. The angelic realm is the place of warfare, from which Satan and his angels fell and from where they seek to invade and take over the earth. It is also the place where the angels of God fight on our behalf, as described by the Lord in Daniel's vision. The Church is called to rise up into this battle because, now seated with Christ in the heavenly places,

> *'...our struggle is not against flesh and blood, but against the rulers, against the powers, against the world forces of this darkness, against the spiritual forces of wickedness in the heavenly places.'*     (Ephesians 6:12)

The epistle to the Ephesians is supremely the book which describes the weapons and practice of spiritual warfare, and the experience of Paul in Ephesus illustrates this. We remember how, when he came into the city the church was as yet unacquainted with the Holy Spirit. Paul addressed this lack immediately, because church is called to function properly at the interface of earth and heaven, and this we must do by the presence and power of the Holy Spirit. For Ephesus was already a spiritually active city in many other senses. Magicians and foreign gods proliferated. Yet the young church was not instructed to avoid these powers, but to enter into confrontation with them. Indeed, the power of God with Paul was manifest so powerfully in this arena that the magician sons of Sceva actually attempted to draw from it themselves, using the name of Jesus and the name of Paul to command demons, who recognised the names, but did not submit to the authority of the men using them! There was also a steady stream of occult practitioners in the city, many of whom came to faith and burned their artefacts. Finally and most significantly, there was in Ephesus the temple of Artemis of the Greeks, known as Diana by the Romans. She was one of the most powerful manifestations of the Queen of Heaven in the New Testament era. Ephesus as a city drew much power and benefit from her being there. She belonged to the city, *'for who does not know that the city of the Ephesians is the guardian of the temple of the great Artemis and of the image which fell down from heaven?'* (Acts 19:35). But they did not understand that cities do not guard goddesses, but goddesses control cities. And this was by their own agreement, for the silversmiths made good trade by selling Artemis images and it was these merchants who were stirred up against Paul and his companions. The whole experience of the gospel coming to this city was that it immediately, boldly and deliberately, contested the powers of darkness already installed in the territory. Paul acknowledged the cost and effort of this confrontation when he wrote that *'he fought with wild beasts at Ephesus'* (1 Corinthians 15:32).

## Compromise

So how did Ephesus become such a place of spiritual strongholds? What had attracted and empowered such an array of demonic manifestations? What were the gateways created on the earth that gave entry to the spiritual powers in the heavenly places over this city? The history of Ephesus reveals a startling incidence of amoral, pragmatic and manipulative agreements. The exorcists wanted to make a name for themselves and would use any power going. The greed motivation of the silversmiths aligned itself with the worship of the Queen of Heaven. The whole atmosphere of the place was one of spiritual compromise and expediency. Compromise sums up the fundamental ground established for the stronghold in the city of Ephesus. And the church had to begin to contest it! They were obviously alert to the territorial pressure to confuse and blur truth and falsehood, so they tested those who made a claim to spiritual authority and leadership and were able to discern right from wrong. They were active, persevering and, very significantly, they were not tolerant of the Nicolaitans, who had caused others of the seven churches to stumble. The Nicolaitans appear to have been a movement within the churches which asserted a hierarchical distinction between the leaders and the 'ordinary members' in direct contradiction to Jesus' words that we should not *'lord it over'* one another (Luke 22:25). They were the earliest evidence of the imperial spirit of Rome beginning to impact or invade the organisation of the Church. The Ephesian believers were even alert to this developing stronghold.

But it is in this context that the Lord warns His people that they must repent from losing their first love and return to it. For good mental and doctrinal practice does not safeguard the Church from compromise. Replacing the law of love, even with the law of truth, leaves us wide open to invasion from the very strongholds that we were called to displace. Even aggressive informed warfare will not keep demonic spirits at bay if they are empowered by expediency and self-interest. They are only overcome by overwhelming passion for Jesus and a readiness to lay down our lives for Him. The compromise of expediency, of alliances of like with unlike for a common goal, where the end justifies the means, created the right atmosphere for the enthronement of Artemis, the Queen of Heaven, in Ephesus. We believe it also sourced the alignment of the Church with the State and facilitated the same enthronement in Europe.

So now we must learn the lesson of the Ephesus gateway. Remember that Jesus holds the angelic realm in His hand and walks among the churches on the earth, making and marking the connection. We will need to fight the same wild beasts that Paul struggled against in the heavenly places, to win them back from the Queen of Heaven. We are called to resist her in the heavens and on the earth. And her earthly ground is compromise. That is why we have to return to our first love, Jesus.

We do not believe that first love means first chrono-logically, with its inference that earlier in the Christian walk they loved Him more than they did latterly. We believe that the experience of the Ephesian believers would have been like that of most committed Christians today, that they love Jesus more today that when they first believed into Him. How else would they be continuing in such perseverance and toil? But as life goes on and the battle continues, there are other demands and pressures to which we must give atten-tion. There is also more glory and more joy. Life gets much fuller. And we love and are committed to many things, good, worthy things. We don't love Jesus less than we did, but we do love other things alongside Him. And our love for Him has to make alliances with our love for success, even break-through. We fail now by sins of omission as we juggle many honourable demands, rather than by commission of deliber-ate acts of rebellion. Compromise empowers the Queen of Heaven. Intimacy with Jesus in the Holy Spirit, in the presence of angels, is the only antidote to compromise.

The 'first deeds' of the Ephesian church were that they were baptised into John's baptism. Without even knowing of the glory of Christ's salvation and the fullness of blessing promised in the Holy Spirit, they did the first deed, which was to make the choice to repent, to turn from anything other than extreme righteousness. They were totally prepared for the Kingdom of God, and to be, like John, prophetic zealots! It is interesting in the light of John the

Baptist's preaching of repentance that the prophecy to the church at Ephesus also refers to repenting as **doing** *'the deeds you did at first.'* Remember how John called for fruits of repentance that could be measured tangibly in changed behaviour?

> *'The multitudes were questioning him saying, "Then what shall we do?" and he would answer and say to them, "Let the man who has two tunics share with him who has none; and let him who has food do likewise."'*
>
> (Luke 3:10–11)

For the Church to be functioning redemptively and authoritatively at the interface of heaven and earth, we must be living on the earth in a truly heavenly manner. Our attitude therefore to the values of the world is hugely important. We will inevitably refer to the issue of wealth in connection with others of the seven letters, but we must flag it here also. The greed of the silversmiths and their trade had made a landing place for Artemis. The repentance preached by John and the Ephesian church's ground for victorious warfare also had to do with living differently from the consumerist, greed-based values of their culture. Nothing has changed. Twenty-first-century Christian has got to return to a first love that is marked by radical living in the areas of justice for the poor and advocacy for the oppressed, and not in word only, but in lifestyle changes as tangible as John described.

## Desert Fathers

It was perhaps this letter that produced the lifestyle example of the desert fathers to whom we referred earlier. These early believers who found themselves unable to live radically in the compromise of Constantinean Christianity, withdrew to the deserts to establish small communities given to asceticism, to prayer and to servanthood. Many came out to them for wisdom and guidance to bring to bear on the increasingly confusing journey of faith in and through the increasing compromise of the Christian religion with the false values and authority of the Roman empire. Most students of these communities would trace their beginnings back to John's apostleship established out of Ephesus and they do perhaps offer us a redemptive pattern, a sign that these words of the Lord were heeded and obeyed. The indigenous Celts of Europe received from this source their marvellous, radical gospel lifestyle, which has been an ancient well of life in many of our lands, though mostly dry or blocked today. With the changing shape of Church called for in our time, thank God that some of us are re-digging these old monastic wells, these signs of extravagant love and alternative wisdom that could challenge forever the compromise and injustice of expedient religiosity!

Repentance, both personal and intercessory, is the key weapon of spiritual warfare. To overcome the strongholds instituted in the gates of our continent, it will not be sufficient to bind and cast them down, but we will need to learn first, as Christ wrote to Ephesus, to repent, to take away the ground, the 'armour in which they trusted', and to cleanse the sin that gave them foundations. Spiritual compromise is deeply offensive to the High King of Heaven. Not because He needs to be flattered as the greatest, but because His commitment to us is total, wholehearted and written in the blood of Jesus. He is worthy of nothing less.

## Smyrna

> *'And to the angel of the church in Smyrna write: The first and the last, who was dead, and has come to life, says this ... "Do not fear what you are about to suffer ... Be faithful until death ... "'*                    (Revelation 2:8, 10)

Smyrna's angel is only encouraged! The church is honoured for her perseverance in the trials of faith and wonderfully, in the light of our last point about greed, is praised for her poverty. These people of God are persevering in the face of opposition from the religious Judaizers, whom the Lord identifies with Satan himself. They are overcoming. They are not called to repent.

But they are warned about fear. And here is our clue to the stronghold that the enemy tries to build to prevent the spread of the vibrant, passionate gospel of the Kingdom. This temptation to fear follows on naturally from the first stronghold formed around a lack of active love and makes a potentially lethal agreement. This stronghold is evident today right across Europe in a theology that draws a veil over the call to suffer for Christ's sake.

Some years ago, I (Sue) was talking to the leader of one of the biggest of the new missions organisations that has seen literally millions of young people flood through the world in outreach and mercy ministry. He was showing me a copy of their newest brochure detailing the projects and schemes in which young Christians could be involved. It was glossy and attractive, offering life experiences and a vast choice of how to participate in short-term mission, providing opportunities which would also look good on their CV. It was persuasive and, in marketing terms, well researched in how to reach potential customers! He smiled somewhat wistfully, remembering the call to the first generation of would-be mission pioneers from his organisation. It was a grey photocopied brochure inviting people to 'Come, Live, Die!' Now, neither we nor he want in any way to criticise the sacrificial and marvellously effective work done by both this mission and many like it, to say nothing of the young men and women who have paid enormous cost in time, money, health, relationships and career to go and live and work among the world's poor and needy! But the parable of the brochure is a telling one. To reach, educate and train today's workforce for God, at least the initial packaging seems to need to be geared to what is on offer, and what is to be gained by involvement in this trip or that experience. Obviously the majority of those who become involved are either already choosing a sacrificial investment in the Kingdom, or are at least open to being subverted by the true gospel of Jesus! But the point is that, for the most part, modern western theology and Christian experience are geared around what this gospel can do for you, not what you can do for Christ or those for whom He died. We fully understand that when Christ called us all He did say,

> *'Come to Me, all you who are weary and heavy laden, and I will give you rest.'*                    (Matthew 11:28)

We know that His yoke is easy and His burden light, but it is also true that 'in your presence, all my problems disappear' is not a song sung easily by intercessors! Yes, there is a freedom that brings release from our own sin and guilt, which is glorious and marvellous and ushers us into God's own presence with singing. But there is also a Christ who, though this same heavenly presence and freedom was His by right, emptied Himself and came to embrace the tortuous cross to take on the sin of those still outside the glory! And there is a Comforter, who even when Christ Himself, the spotless, glorious manifestation of all goodness was despised and rejected by humankind, was still poured out onto all flesh to suffer again each time we grieve Him or quench His moving in and through all of creation!

## Fear of Death

Since *'there is no fear in love, but perfect love casts out fear'* (1 John 4:18), the opposite is also true. Lack of love will give place to fear. A lack of abandoned, 'unreasonable' passion for Jesus and for all that He is passionate about, even while holding true to sound doctrine, will leave us vulnerable to fear. Indeed, the stronghold of all human life is that we are those *'who through fear of death were subject to slavery all their lives'* (Hebrews 2:15). And Christ came to deliver us from this. That is why He warns those in Smyrna who, in the heat of the battle between His gracious, free offer of deliverance and the legalistic accusation of religious authorities, may well be called on to lay down their lives just as He did, not to be afraid! He does not encourage them to believe that they will, with all intercession, prayer, fasting and warfare, with enough faith, definitely be able to win the victory and be delivered from death. His promise is that, in that death, He is the One who is able to deliver them from the second death! The death that holds us all in bondage. The death that is to do with punishment. If *'love is perfected with us ... we may have confidence in the day of judgement; because as He is, so also are we in this world'* (1 John 4:17), we can be faithful even in the face of the death of the body, because, if we are, we cannot be hurt by the second death of judgement. And if we are not captive to the fear of the death of judgement, why should we fear death at all? Indeed, it is those who overcome in exactly this test that may aspire even to the first resurrection, the out-resurrection from among the dead! With Paul we are encouraged to press on to know Him *'and the power of His resurrection and **the fellowship of His sufferings**, being conformed to His death; in order that I may attain to the resurrection from the dead'* (Philippians 3:10, our emphasis).

It was a daunting experience to hear the ministry of 'The Heavenly Man', a pastor who has connection with some 80 million Christians in China. He has finally had to leave his country, bidden to do so by an angel, in order to help those of us in the western nations to understand more fully the calling of the gospel. His plea to us is not to pray that the persecution of the Chinese believers cease, but that they may stand in and through it. It is in the testing of faith that it is proved and strengthened. Miracles are commonplace in this atmosphere of complete confidence. Suffering is not necessarily to be sought, but neither is it to be feared. Where we are conformed to His sufferings, we are also promised to share in His glory.

It is our conviction that the fear of suffering has a strong and stifling grip on our European experience of the gospel. In the face of this fear, the Catholic Church has to some extent glorified a passive acceptance of evil experience as the permissive will of God, which followers are encouraged to embrace as somehow purging of sin and guilt. In this way, the fact that followers of an all-powerful and all-loving God suffer can be explained. But this undermines the power and glory of the once-for-all sacrifice of the Son of God to deal with all sin and guilt. Evangelicals and particularly Charismatics, on the other hand, have leaned towards a denial of suffering as a valid part of our present experience. All healing, forgiveness, blessing and welfare are now available in Christ and lack of the full experience of all this, with prosperity, is a mark of lack of faith. But the obedience of faith must find us in a war zone where neither passive acceptance nor strident denial avail a great deal. Intercessory suffering, the necessary cost payable by the people of God living and loving in a world resistant to the revelation of the glory and image of the Saviour, is expected of the church in Smyrna. But even understanding this is not necessarily going to equip us to pay the price. We have to be fully delivered from the fear of deathly judgement! We have to have a gospel experience that is truly resurrection based and a clear conviction that we follow the One who *'was dead and has come to life'* (Revelation 2:8). We have to have already done the deal to give up our own lives in this cause, in order that we may take them up again!

As John Mulinde led many in Uganda in intercession for their nation, he realised he had to take them into a covenant that 'whether by life or by death' they were given to God for the redemption of their land. In the European context we know many who react to that statement. How could their death or the offer of it have any effect on the nation? Isn't such a statement potentially a negative confession, inviting the possibility of death and as such giving ground to the devil who has the power of death? Indeed, how arrogant it seems that such an offer would even be necessary, given that Christ died once for all, so that now we can live! There is no question that our willingness to give up our lives in prayer and longing for the salvation of a land can in any way be atoning for that land. This is and was the unique effect of Jesus' suffering. Yet He called us into the same lifestyle, to a death to our own fleshly desires and expectations, to a life of pressure, struggle and persecution!

*'If anyone wishes to come after Me, let him deny himself and take up his cross and follow Me. For whoever wishes to save his life shall lose it; but whoever loses his life for My sake shall find it.'* (Matthew 16:24)

And His teaching was very clear that we would be required to risk persecution and antagonism. Martyrdom was and is a very real possibility for some believers, and with it comes the most overwhelming victory!

*'You will be delivered up even by parents and brothers and relatives and friends and they will put some of you to death and you will be hated by all on account of My name. Yet not a hair of your head will perish. By your endurance you will gain your lives.'* (Luke 21:16–19)

Delivered up to death but not a hair perishing? Willingness freely to give up our lives, being faithful even to physical death, delivers us from the second death!

## Showing Forth His Death

But some may still question this. Has not Jesus' vicarious death already saved us from the death of judgement? When we believe into Him, do we not pass from death to life and receive the promise that we shall not see death? This is certainly orthodox belief, but so too is scriptural teaching on the call to suffer with Him, to make up in our own body the suffering of Christ. To reconcile these two positions, therefore, it may be necessary to define our believing into Him as our willingness to suffer with Him! And this is where we suspect that the stronghold of the fear of suffering has been set up in Europe. We simply do not have a vibrant enough theology of suffering to equip us to stand in the fiery trial. Most of us have not even begun to submit to the discipline of the gospel in struggling through to a place of personal holiness, let alone being prepared to suffer the same hostility and antagonism that the author of our faith drew against Himself (Hebrews 12:2–4)! In John's Gospel, when Jesus spoke these awesome words about His cross, it was in the context of overcoming or casting out Satan himself.

> *'And I, if I be lifted up from the earth, will draw all to Myself.'*                    (John 12:32)

Often translated 'all men', the drawing power of the cross is, in fact, of all things. It is in this way that Jesus is reconciling *'all things to Himself ... through the blood of His cross'* (Colossians 1:20). His willingness to die, His open demonstration of a self-giving love that is stronger than death, is a plumbline throughout the heavens and the earth, to which all things must come to be measured. His goodness literally commands the attention and disclosure of the heart and attitude of all, including the devil himself. The light and revelation of His freely given life is the eternal standard by which all things are measured and, without redemption, are found wanting. When we are commanded to take up our cross and follow Him, we are called to the same dynamic. Declaring and identifying with His willingness to die convicts everything not made in the same glorious image. It is a lifestyle destined to provoke all manner of opposition! It deliberately drew death itself to Christ and as He was, so are we in the world.

In these days of post-Christian Europe, it may well be that the days of favour for the gospel are passing through mere tolerance to antagonism. This may be both our worst nightmare and our finest hour. To invest in the latter and be saved from the former, we will need to lay hold fully of the revelation that the angel of Smyrna received of the awesome resurrection power of the Lord Jesus and hope and pray to attain to that. We must resist all fear of suffering and break the stronghold of a 'bless-me' theology and shallow passive triumphalism. It is time to *'go out to Him outside the camp, bearing His reproach'* (Hebrews 13:13). It is time to fill up the symbol of the communion and by our poured-out lives *'proclaim the Lord's death until He comes'* (1 Corinthians 11:26).

## Pergamum

> *'And to the angel of the church in Pergamum write: The One who has the sharp two-edged sword says this ... "I have a few things against you, because you have some who hold the teaching of Balaam ... [and] some who in the same way hold the teaching of the Nicolaitans."'*

Failure to engage properly in the struggle of the gospel, both in our personal lives as we put *'to death the deeds of the body'* (Romans 8:13) and in our corporate lives as we live confrontationally among the darkened values and corrupt choices of the cultures of the world, will lead to another level of demonisation. In the lack of passionate, abandoned love for Jesus and His world, a secret unspoken fear of judgement takes root. Then, again often unspoken, an agreement in the felt need to be sheltered from this fear creates the demand for another form of righteousness, a body of teaching to establish a structural, institutional definition in which to hide. The story of Balaam is a complex one, but it was the fear in Moab and Balak that caused them to plead for a word, a teaching from God via Balaam that would protect them from God's judgement (see Numbers 22–25). The word of God was not to protect them from fear of death. It could teach them of the need to fear and turn to Him rather than try to turn Him away from His own will and way! But in the face of the need of their flesh to be comforted and protected, Balaam chose rather to identify with them than with the word of God so clearly and majestically spoken to him. He made this choice because his own fleshly desires had not been put to the sword. His secret heart found a resonance with the natural desires of Moab rather than an answering chord with the two-edged sword of God's perfect word of love and discipline. His inner man was *'trained in greed'* (2 Peter 2:14) rather than trained in God's goodness, so for all his outward righteousness and perfect teaching, *'the way of truth* [was] *maligned...'* (2 Peter 2:2) and many followed his sensuality!

In Pergamum, God honours those who have overcome in the battle against fear, for in this city, where Satan's throne is, it has been required of Antipas to lay down his life for Christ. His sacrifice has strengthened some in their faith, but has provoked others in their sensuality, and these have been legitimised in their fleshly choices by false teaching after the manner of Balaam. How is it that Balaam who, by biblical record, never uttered a false word, can be held responsible for continually teaching Balak to stumble the people of God into immorality and idolatry? Because as a leader and bearer of God's word, he played fast and loose in his own life. He spoke and held sound doctrine, but guarded the idol of wealth and reputation in his heart. He incarnated double-mindedness and released it in the earth. He patterned using the revelation of God to his own ends rather than for the blessing of all the families of the earth. So his teaching was false teaching, *'holding to a form of godliness, although ...* [denying] *its power'* (2 Timothy 3:5). It was not in any sense good teaching, though correct in its form. It was deadly and destructive. It was the preaching of the letter of the law which kills, rather than the ministry of the Spirit in and through the Word of God which brings life. We have been so proud of our teaching in Europe. And yet we must consider whether we might be guilty of holding the teaching of Balaam. Certainly as we considered in the early chapters, the historical pattern of our outreach into all the earth had a distinct Balaamite quality about it! Seeking to do the godly thing, taking the truth of the gospel into all the earth, we discovered with hindsight the pollution of much of this activity in the aftermath of the colonial era. We wonder if we might, as sensitively as possible, raise an issue which might illustrate that this effect of double-mindedness and self-serving continues in our thinking and practice today.

# Tithing

In a remarkably brave paper entitled 'Embezzlement: the Corporate Sin of Contemporary Christianity?' Ray Mayhew traces the theological thinking necessary in the transition from Jewish Law to New Testament practice concerning the giving and use of the tithe. He points out that the parallels made between the Church in the New Testament and the Old Testament Jewish structures are often a mismatch. In the Old Testament the tithe was given to the Levites, 'a tribe', Mayhew points out, 'to which those who gave did not belong. In contrast, when I give to the church, it is not "given away" at all. I am the church!' He goes on to propose that even if we parallel Old Testament priests with New Testament clergy or pastoral staff (another tenuous link) they would only qualify to receive 'a tithe of the tithe' (Nehemiah 12:47). The point is this: we have thought only superficially about what is involved in bringing our tithe into the Lord's house.

Mayhew suggests:

> 'At this point it will be helpful to stand in the shoes of an early Jewish convert. Jews throughout the Empire already had a "culture of tithing". However, as Jewish converts slowly began to be alienated from both the synagogue and temple, one of their obvious perplexities was where to give the tithe. (Not that the tithe was seen as a legal necessity, but it continued to provide a good benchmark of faithful stewardship.) Obviously it would be given to the church. However, the big question was, what does the church do with it now that there is no longer a Levitical tribe to maintain?
>
> This was no easy decision to make. Church funds were not seen simply as revenue to be spent as needed. The incident with Ananias and Sapphira was an indicator on how seriously they viewed the issue. Their decision to use it primarily to bridge the chasm between the "haves" and the "have nots" ... is well known.

However, **why** they chose to do this was a deeply
theological decision. It had to be. In the issue of sacred
revenue they were conscious of standing on holy
ground and handling holy things...

Their decision to give it to those degraded by hunger
and disease had a huge evangelistic impact but this was
not the motivation for their actions. However pressing
the need or valid the cause, the tithe was not seen as
theirs by right to redirect as needed. They understood it
as belonging to the poor by right. The bulk of their
funds did not even go into the missionary enterprise for
which they both lived and laid down their lives – it
went to those lacking the basic necessities of life.
They were examining Scripture in the light of Christ
and it was reshaping their understanding of justification, the Law, the prophets, the temple, the priesthood
– and the tithe. Their conclusion that it should now
be given to the weak and destitute was as considered
and weighty as Paul's in defining the doctrine of
justification.'

Our present, pretty well general understanding of tithing is
that the first ten per cent of our disposable income should go
to the local church or denomination where it will probably
be used to salary pastoral staff, to care for the spiritual needs
of individuals and their families, to meet the costs of buildings and of the administration of ancillary projects, good
worthy projects into the locality. This seems to differ hugely
from the intensively thoughtful process that led to sacrificial
giving for the poor in the early days of an inspirationally-
led Church. A restored understanding that our tithes are
primarily destined by the Lord for the poor will indeed have
enormous repercussions. How will we fund all the activities
of a local church structure? But perhaps we should not begin
with questions about pragmatic costs and expenditure, but
peel back to underlying questions of the nature of the tithe in
the first place. Essentially, it is because God is for the poor,
His good news is for the oppressed, and He is burdened for

those who are disempowered. Therefore, throughout the Old Testament Law, the giving of alms was considered as the primary act of devotion to God Himself because in caring for the poor we are identifying with God's own heart.

> 'The Jews used the word *zedakah* both for righteousness and almsgiving. Giving alms and being righteous were considered one and the same thing. Jesus endorsed this and used it as the criteria in separating the sheep and the goats at the end of the age.'

To bring the whole tithe into God's storehouse as He commanded in Malachi 3 was to bring the fruits of repentance, a sign of turning from self-orientated religion. Religious practice of tithing and teaching that puts my church and me and my needs at the centre leaves the poor uncared for and the destitute without help or hope in the world, and the last state is even worse than the first. The poor are still poor and unrelieved. The rich now add hypocrisy to their sins. True and undefiled religion is *'to visit orphans and widows in their distress and to keep oneself unstained by the world'* (James 1:27) and it is this that we are called to as followers of Jesus. Malachi berates the people of God for talking emptily about His blessing while they themselves are not concerned about the needs of the poor. He therefore warns them strongly, because God is *'"against those who oppress the wage earner in his wages, the widow and the orphan, and those who turn aside the alien, and do not fear Me," says the Lord of hosts'* (Malachi 3:5) and requires an immediate change of heart marked by bringing the tithe as alms for the poor.

Yet so often when we are referred to this passage about tithing, we are assured that to bring our tenth into the house of God will cause Him to open the windows of heaven and pour down His blessing on us, even to the multiplying of our income. How did it become circular like this? I bless God's house, which incidentally exists to bless me and then God will also bless me again? Bringing the tithe was a sign of turning from exactly that attitude, a mark that I was turning my heart away from myself and my comfort and being conformed to the likeness of Christ in His care for those lacking the basics of life! Surely this is an example of the teaching of Balaam, where the very truth of Scripture, sounding so doctrinally secure, actually issues in the very opposite of that for which it was spoken. It comes from an unregenerate value system informing the hearing of God's Word, and, finding an answering chord in the unreformed world-view of the hearer; it puts a *'stumbling block before the sons of Israel'* and causes many *'to commit acts of immorality'* (Revelation 2:14).

There are certainly answers to the practical questions of resourcing the affairs of the church by other means than tithing. And it is certainly not our intent to criticise or dishonour any who give sacrificially to God's work, or indeed those who live by their gifts in their acts of service. God knows the heart and the work and the need and the faithfulness. But we are facing a window of opportunity in Europe to reconsider the means whereby we lost the glorious presence of God from walking and talking with us in the streets and cities of our continent. Only radical and provoking consideration of some root issues, some hitherto unchallenged corporate paradigms, will be enough to redeem the years. We will need to let the sharp two-edged sword of the Lord separate to the dividing point of soul and spirit, to seek out the places where we hold the double-minded, self-serving false teaching of Balaam.

## Issues of Authority

And what of the teaching of the Nicolaitans? The Greek root of the word seems to mean the separation of the people (*laos*) from the leaders who rule over or conquer (*nico*) them. By the Lord's own words, these are teachings and deeds which He hates. As we described earlier, Jesus in the days of His flesh was specific about forms of leadership which, even in the name of being beneficial, are also at root self-serving.

> *'The kings of the Gentiles lord it over them; and those who
> have authority over them are called "Benefactors". But not
> so with you, but let him who is the greatest among you
> become as the youngest and the leader as the servant. For
> who is greater, the one who reclines at the table, or the one
> who serves? Is it not the one who reclines at the table? But I
> am among you as the one who serves.'*     (Luke 22:25–27)

Now Jesus in His resurrection power is even more unyield-
ing on this issue! Leadership which has the concept of
'conquering' in it, of taking a powerful position over and
against another who is thereby dis-empowered, even when
exercised from the best motives, is contributing to a fallen
mindset and structure which carries its own pollution. He
hates it! It is inimical to the content of the gospel where
He who was in the very form of God emptied and humbled
Himself, becoming totally powerless in every way, except
that granted by the presence of the Holy Spirit at work in and
through Him. He came with no official weight of authority
which separated Him out from others. Quite the opposite!
Why else was He born in a stable, and made a sign to the
shepherds by being wrapped in cloths? Powerlessness person-
ified! Delivered up, bound, in life and in death. He had no
beauty that we should desire Him. He did not lift up His
voice in the street and cry aloud, demanding our attention.
He would not allow them to come and make Him king, but
slipped away and hid Himself. It seemed unreasonable,
unworthy and impractical behaviour, given His vision and
mandate to save the whole world! Even His disciples did not
really believe He meant to continue this way. Surely, finally,
His kingship would be revealed and then they could sit
on His right hand and left. Their whole discussion was about
how to sort out the pecking order for the moment when Jesus
had achieved all He came to gain through this winsome
humility and got on with the real business of ruling and
reigning. Servanthood is all very well, but surely a means to
an end. After all, after He became low and obedient, He was
exalted to the right hand of the Father. When we've passed

the test, surely we also get to be officially in charge! It is interesting to note that while 'Nicolaitan' in the Greek means 'conquering the people', Balaam means this in the Hebrew! Double-mindedness rears its head here also. To serve others in a way that ends up with us being served is to lead people astray. Forgive our brutality, but don't we need to recognise the deceitfulness of the flesh in all this?

## God's Servant Nature

Peter did get his heart's desire to be a leader like Jesus.

> *'Truly, truly I say to you, when you were younger, you used to gird yourself, and walk wherever you wished; but when you grow old, you will stretch out your hands, and someone else will gird you, and bring you where you do not want to go.'*
> (John 21:18)

In his maturity he would be marked with the same powerlessness. And James and John do get to drink the cup that Jesus would drink in His glory. For His glory is that He *'did not come to be served, but to serve, and to give His life a ransom for many'* (Mark 10:45). The very nature of Jesus is that He always was the Lamb slain from the foundation of the earth, and continues forever to be the servant of all. So even at the end of all things, it is still that Lamb who is enthroned. He is not servant while in the form of man just to put humanity back in its rightful, subordinate place and then God who calls the shots when restored to heaven. *'God was in Christ, reconciling the world to Himself'* (2 Corinthians 5:19). Jesus in the flesh was and is the exact representation of the Father's glory. Now ascended, there is a man in heaven. Called to this same kind of authority, born of the same nature, redeemed humankind is also to be poured out to release, serve and facilitate others just as Jesus has released us and served us with His life. We are raised to exert power over all the works of unrighteousness, not one another. We are authorised to command the devil to submit to us, not one another. We are equipped to master the sin that is crouching at the door, not to have the mastery over our brothers and sisters, our equals, our co-heirs.

## Accountability

So how does true godly leadership and authority work, while avoiding the hated stronghold of the conquering or dominating Nicolaitan teaching, since we do not want to throw the baby of right leadership out with the bath water of fallen practice? As with holding the teaching of Balaam, it is not likely to be a question of correct doctrine to be believed, but of heart attitudes and desires and in this respect we are sure that most Christian leaders in Europe today earnestly desire to serve those in their care. Yet we have to acknowledge that there does seem to be a vast discrepancy between the active engagement of most (rather tired) leaders in the European Church and the somewhat remarkable passivity of the majority of people sitting in the churches on a Sunday morning. There is, for all our care, an imbalance of engagement. A relatively few, usually vocal, leaders seem empowered, and by contrast the majority of the body seem disempowered. Relatively few, usually vocal, leaders are setting the vision, the agenda and dictating the activity and, by contrast, a large majority are at best compliant, following and co-operative, at worst disengaged but dependent. Who or what might be the reason?

It appears to us that in the negotiating of forms and structures in the church, a transfer of responsibility takes place between those termed leaders and the rest. We negotiate with the leader that he or she will be responsible for certain tasks and ideas, indeed take on a fairly complex role, and in return the body will give support, be it financial, our physical presence when required or at least our agreement. Perhaps it is a relief to have been able to delegate that responsibility and now we can concern ourselves with other things. But for many of us, church has actually come to represent the main expression of our faith! How can we

delegate that responsibility? Now in 'normal life', the opposite happens. In 'normal life', the process of growth and
development leads us to be ready to take on more and more
responsibility, especially in those areas that mean the most
to us. We take on more and more responsibility in relationships: we marry and bear multiple children for whom we
choose to be responsible. We invest in property, business,
education, community, and the more we invest, the more we
exercise due care, thought, prayer, energy. Why does the
opposite seem to happen in the area of our primary calling,
that of knowing God and making Him known?

It seems to do with our expectations that in this arena we
are required to show our spiritual grace by being submissive.

> *'Obey your leaders and submit to them; for they keep watch
> over your souls, as those who will give an account. Let them
> do this with joy and not with grief, for this would be
> unprofitable for you.'*                      (Hebrews 13:17)

Again and again we hear questions about 'Who is your
covering?' or 'To whom are you accountable?' And because
we see Jesus, struggling with His own flesh in the garden of
Gethsemane, pressing through to victory with those marvellous words, *'Yet not my will, but thine, be done'*, we have come
to believe that the highest value in the Kingdom is laying
down our own will and desires, and pattern that by finding
someone in a leadership role to whom we can lay them
down. But we would like to suggest that there are some
serious weaknesses in this arrangement which make us very
vulnerable, both as leaders and as those not currently
functioning in church leadership, to the stronghold of a
Nicolaitan spirit.

Firstly, it implies stereotypical behaviour, that some people
groups should act in one way and others differently. Now
there are various people categories that are instructed to obey
or submit in the Scriptures: wives are told to obey their
husbands and children their parents; slaves are enjoined to
be obedient to their masters (Ephesians 5:22–6:6); and in the

Hebrew in the verses just quoted, non-leaders are required to obey leaders. But if we hold these verses as proof texts for set behaviour patterns we do great damage to the meaning and purpose of the Scripture. Because we also read that we are all to submit to one another (Ephesians 5:21). We are taught that in Christ there are, in fact, no longer any category distinctions (Galatians 3:28), and we are enjoined 'do not submit!' (to a yoke of slavery) (Galatians 5:1). Jesus Himself tells us not to be called 'Rabbi' *'because One is your Teacher and you are all brothers ... And do not be called leaders; for One is your leader, that is, Christ'* (Matthew 23:8, 10).

So this position fails to recognise process or progress, but sees these scriptures as eternally fixed and universally true. If they are fixed, then they are contradictory, as we have seen above. If they are not contradictory, as we believe they cannot be, then they are to be applied contextually. For instance, do we really believe that slaves should forever be obedient to masters? Self apparently not, because while Paul was writing to the slaves, to help them find how to live prophetically and gloriously out of heaven in a tragically demonic world system, he was also working to see that Christians must change the circumstances too. So Onesimus is sent back to Philemon as a brother, which would have subsumed the previous relationship of master/slave. Are wives always and forever to be subject to their husbands? If the image is that this is an eternal hierarchical pattern in the same shape as God is head of Christ (1 Corinthians 11:3), what exactly does this imply? For God and Christ are one and forever equal and the same, except in the limited context of Christ emptying Himself for the purpose of salvation. As long as there is a need for us to be saved from fallen patterning and sin, it may be necessary to subject ourselves **voluntarily** (as Jesus freely chose to come to die), while sin patterns in the flesh are put to death. But these are mutual arrange-ments. Ephesians 5 sets the context more clearly to illustrate this. Wives and husbands are both called to love one another (v. 1) and submit to one another (v. 21). But then wives are enjoined to submit to husbands, as to the Lord (this is really important, or we may find ourselves insisting on subjection to an abusive bully!) and husbands are told to love their wives. If there are any particular sin patterns that need taking to the cross to be emptied out, it may be the following. As Eve was tempted in the garden by the serpent, she failed to trust her husband fully and submit to his wisdom. (Check out Genesis 1 and 2. It seems she was not even formed when God gave Adam the instructions about what and what not to eat, so she may have been more vulnerable by only having second-hand revelation of God's mind and intent.) But was Adam's reaction that bright? She had eaten from the tree of the knowledge of good and evil, and he simply joined in, rather than racing her immediately into the Lord's presence and repenting that he may not have made the instructions clear enough! His failure was a lack of committed love. So a Christian wife is encouraged to submit to trusting a godly husband while he commits to be more consciously and actively loving. Both weaknesses are drained of their power. And when the fleshly patterning has submitted to the disciplines? The marriage is a strong partnership of equals, to express the image of Christ rising again to God's right hand, His rightful and eternal place, and, indeed, Christ welcoming His bride, for whom He died, to His great marriage supper! The context has changed and different instructions apply. Creative relationships that address particular issues and weaknesses in us must surely be for a season only, or we lock one another into dependent relationships. We become passive if we never grow out of the particular category and function as a responsible individual.

And this is the end and the purpose for which Christ came. To those who overcome this temptation to co-dependent relationships, the promise is that Jesus will give *'hidden manna'* and *'a new name written which no one knows but he who receives it'* (Revelation 2:17). The role of individual responsibility to hear from Him who has the sword of revelation is given to us all. Accountability to anything other than that is idolatry.

Christians are all called to be leaders. To lead others into faith and relationship with Christ. To lead their children, their partners, their workmates, their neighbours into hope and righteousness. People are called to be free and to hold themselves accountable before God to fulfil their calling and destiny. We all have a responsibility to lay hold of any and every gift given to the body of Christ to build us up in the most holy faith. When we honour the gift and calling in another, we honour God. When we lay down the responsibility to develop the gift and calling in our own life, we dishonour the God who gave it. Let us walk out of Nicolaitan strongholds and commit to walking in the freedom for which Christ has set us free.

## Thyatira

> *'And to the angel of the church in Thyatira write: The Son of God who has eyes like a flame of fire, and His feet are like burnished bronze, says this: "I have this against you, that you tolerate the woman Jezebel . . . "'* (Revelation 2:18, 20)

The church in Thyatira was an astonishing community by the sound of it. The Lord knew that their actions were the sure evidence of their *'love and faith and service and perseverance'*, and that this was getting better all the time. It sounds as if the maturity in Thyatira could not be faulted. However, experience shows that the devil lays his biggest plans for city churches like this that threaten his kingdom. So his strategy was to establish *'the deep things of Satan'* in Thyatira. And this can logically be done the most easily in a process where fear has replaced love, false teaching is set in place and people are not engaged in active responsibility! This is where false prophecy and domination can actually be set up overtly. As before in the history of the people of God, this meant that it was time to establish the demonic stronghold of Jezebel. That *'the woman Jezebel'* refers to a spiritual stronghold and not just or necessarily a literal woman is born out by both previous and subsequent history. Right at the key time for restoration and recovery for the Kingdom of God in Old Testament days, the days of Elijah, the original Jezebel emerged (1 Kings 16:31). She proved extremely difficult to shift, and even when Jehu eventually instigated her death, the spirit behind her and those with whom she was in satanic collusion continued. It is this ongoing spiritual stronghold that we refer to as the Jezebel spirit and which they encountered in Thyatira. This is the same spirit that we come up against so often blocking the work of the Kingdom of God today. It is specifically a political spirit and uses religion to open the doors for the kingdom of darkness. And it works in partnership with the Queen of Heaven, a religious spirit that uses political power to pursue its ends. We have already seen from our study of Zechariah 5 that these two spirits work together to increase and establish the bounds of Babylonic and anti-God civilisation. In the important booklet *The Three Battlegrounds* (New Wine Press, 1994), Francis Frangipane documents his encounter with this stronghold in the context of seeking to establish the work of the Kingdom of God, which he calls 'the house of the Lord', in a city. It is not difficult to detail the basic characteristics of the Jezebel spirit. They are clearly discernible, both from the Old Testament and from the New Testament perspective.

## Characteristics of the Jezebel Spirit

There are altogether seven aspects describing this stronghold in the Scriptures: idolatry and witchcraft (Revelation 2:20; 1 Kings 18:19; 2 Kings 9:22), sexual immorality (Revelation 2:20–21), resistance to true prophets (1 Kings 19:1–2), false prophecy (Revelation 2:20), control (1 Kings 21:5–7, 11), disinheritance (*'leads My bondservants astray'*, Revelation 2:20; 1 Kings 21:15–16) and murder (1 Kings 19:1; 21:14). These are common aspects of the manifestation of the world, the flesh and the devil. But when they all come together in one place we can be sure that it is Jezebel that we are encountering. It is important to note that a stronghold is in view here, and when we refer to the Jezebel spirit, strictly speaking we are describing people giving way to and partnering with the Jezebel spirit. Otherwise the Lord would not speak of repentance in this connection. Satan and his demons are not called to repent in the Scripture, since they are beyond it. But humans in alliance with Satan form a stronghold by their repeated actions, and by the grace of God they can repent. But like Ananias and Sapphira they can also move beyond repentance (see Acts 5). This terrifying account in the New Testament indicates that we can put ourselves beyond redemption, that even on this glory side of the cross we can face the Lord up with the same dilemma that the Canaanites posed. What is He to do with people and their heirs who steadfastly continue in opposition to everything that the gospel is about, so that the rightful heirs of the promise are disinherited? The Lord's decree is unequivocal in this case:

> *'Behold, I will cast her upon a bed of sickness, and those who commit adultery with her into great tribulation, unless they repent of her deeds. And I will kill her children with pestilence...'* (Revelation 2:22–23)

Our challenge now as then is to overcome these powers that are so inimical to God's Kingdom that they destroy it and at the same time bring destruction on themselves. We need to save both the protagonists and the victims from such destruction.

Now we recognise that by the time we are facing up to the overt establishment of a Jezebelic stronghold in these cites of the early churches, it has been built on layers of foundations. For a citadel of this strength to be set up, there must have been many false and unclean agreements made in the earth. We as the Church will and must attack such strongholds, but from the ground as well as in the spiritual places. This is why the Lord is depicted as having feet like burnished bronze. We have to walk on the earth through the fiery trials of temptation as He did, in order to grow in authority in the heavens.

By the time Jezebel is enthroned, she can act in all the ways listed above, and these become normative practices under her jurisdiction. By living in the opposite spirit and being totally guarded about the 'seeds that grow the trees', we can eat away at the power base of this monstrosity.

Witchcraft and idolatry are full-grown fruits of small beginnings and they work together. Most of us are used to quoting *'rebellion is as the sin of divination, and insubordination is as iniquity and idolatry'* (1 Samuel 15:23). We in Christ must safeguard against attitudes of lawlessness, especially in a post-modern culture. But the warning is in context, and we must use discernment in order to know how to avoid falling into these sinful attitudes.

> *'Has the Lord as much delight in burnt offerings and*
>   *sacrifices*
> *As in obeying the voice of the Lord?*
> *Behold, to obey is better than sacrifice,*
> *And to heed better than the fat of rams.'*
>
> (1 Samuel 15:22)

Fulfilling religious practice or codes of behaviour (sacrifices) will not qualify us as obedient. Only hearing the word of God Himself and obeying it qualifies. Passive compliance to others is not the antidote to rebellion. Indeed, it can be idolatrous! Hungering for God's word and fulfilling it is our safe ground.

Sexual immorality is so powerful for the enemy because it breaks and distorts the image that God created to express His own covenant love. Demons feed on it greedily, but many fall into it originally because of generational strongholds and damage to their own view of God's image in early life. There is plenty of grace for those who repent and lay hold of the healing love of the heavenly Father! But the cause of the original broken relationships may lie elsewhere.

> *'For where jealousy and selfish ambition exist, there is disorder and every vile thing.'*  (James 3:16)

The empowerment for a Jezebelic stronghold, which manifests frequently in sexual immorality, is jealousy. Ahab was jealous of Naboth's vineyard. Jealousy is the root of disinheritance also, and of control. Jezebel was jealous of humble Naboth's ability to resist King Ahab's will. Such jealousy is called covetousness in Old Testament language and it was the original sin of Satan himself. If we are warring against a Jezebelic influence in our city or church, we should let the eyes of Christ search our hearts radically for this root seed! Where any jealous attitude is detected, we must repent and go the second mile. Pray for those by whom you are provoked! Call down all the blessings of heaven on them! Do not seek to take their inheritance, be it their goods, their reputation or their position, but heap goodness over and above. Overcome evil with good.

Prophecy is not easy to handle. It is not intended to be. The nature of prophecy is to disturb, to stir up, to bring about change. It usually draws out a resistance, because not many of us like change. Resistance does not necessarily imply a controlling spirit, or a Jezebelic stronghold. But where the resistance becomes antagonism, where the opposition is bitter and prolonged, this is likely to be what we are encountering. It will lead to murder. But Jesus said that, if we are angry with our brother, then we are guilty of murder also. We must be those who nurture a gentle and quiet spirit, and learn to *'be angry'*, with all the works of the devil, *'and yet ... not sin'* (Ephesians 4:26). The energy of our warfare is to be passionate love for Jesus and His love for righteousness. Anger is a God-given wellspring of energy to overcome evil but if it masters us, we will feed the stronghold of Jezebel's murderous intent, rather than overcome it.

But, not surprisingly, overcoming such a stronghold as this has great rewards for the victory of the Kingdom of God! It is nothing less than spiritual authority over the powers that control nations and the ability to shatter satanic strongholds. This is worth battling for! It includes the stupendous promise that to those who overcome Jezebel *'I will give ... the morning star'* (Revelation 2:28). The morning star was originally Satan's possession and position. Isaiah the prophet addresses him as such in his description of his original fall. Speaking first of the contemporary Babylon of his day, he then begins to address Satan who has come to inhabit the city:

> *'How you have fallen from heaven, O star of the morning, son of the dawn!'*                              (Isaiah 14:12)

This exegesis is borne out by Jesus who later exclaims, *'I was watching Satan fall from heaven like lightening!'* (Luke 10:18). Later, Jesus describes Himself as the morning star.

> *'I am the root and the offspring of David, the bright morning star.'*                                      (Revelation 22:16)

These three parallel uses of the description 'morning star' have enormous implications. Firstly, Satan had the rightful use of the title. This accords with John's description of him as *'ruler of this world'* (John 12:31; 14:30; *passim*). Some people say that this was man's original position and that he surrendered it to Satan at the Fall. We understand the point but we do not hold it. The description of 'morning star' and 'ruler' signifies a rightful rule in the heavenly places over the earth, a responsibility with the other angels and archangels to *'render service for the sake of those who will inherit salvation'* (Hebrews 1:14). This was the position that Satan lost at his fall when he chose to set up and serve the purposes of his own kingdom, leaving the heavenly places in the hands of a rebel power and the peoples of the earth at risk of being subverted and manipulated until they joined him in forming rebel power bases against God. Jesus came to take back the heavenly places and did so on the cross where He *'disarmed the rulers and authorities'* (Colossians 2:15). Hence He is now the 'morning star'. It follows that Jesus has won back the position that Satan had originally held but subverted. Now the people of God can overcome Satanic strongholds in the battle for the cities and nations once again. For Jesus, the title 'morning star' describes a lesser position than the one that He originally had with the Father and the Holy Spirit. But He gained it in order to retrieve it from Satan. The plan, however, was to give the title to overcoming men and women, the kind described by John with the words:

> *'And they overcame him because of the blood of the Lamb and because of the word of their testimony, and they did not love their life even unto death.'* (Revelation 12:11)

This means that the Lord is looking for people who will rise up and be the morning star of our times, standing before God between the heavens and the earth and resisting the rule of Satan.

Some years ago we had a tangle with this stronghold, which, as we have seen in earlier chapters, is endemic in both Church and society in Europe. We make no claim to ultimate victory over it, or any other stronghold in our own strength. Only the risen Christ has that. But we gladly boast of victory in Him. He taught us to war against the pressure in our lives to fear and to anger. To overcome the temptation to doubt the prophetic leading of God or to give way to bitterness in the circumstances in which we felt disinherited. He insisted we made full and frank confession daily to Him of our own sin, and that we bless anyone we could think of who may have had anything against us, or against whom we had sinned. He also broke bread with us every day! Afterwards a Brazilian prophet who spoke no English and knew nothing about us in the natural, prophesied to us out of an open vision. He saw us bound in chains by Queen Jezebel who confronted us, leading a lion on a lead on each hand. Each time the chains were put on us we shook them off, laughing all the time. In the end she turned and left, taking the lions with her. The prophet went on to speak of great victories that would ensue. The same will be true for all who overcome Jezebel. It was not that we were reviling the devil or his demons; the laughter was like that of the Lord in Psalm 2:

> *'The kings of the earth take their stand,*
> *And the rulers take counsel together*
> *Against the Lord and against His Anointed . . .*
> *He who sits in the heavens laughs,*
> *The Lord scoffs at them.*
> *Then He will speak to them in His anger*
> *And terrify them in his fury:*
> *"But as for Me I have installed My King*
> *Upon Zion, My holy mountain." '*                        (vv. 2, 4–6)

Why the laughter? It is the laugh of authority and the laugh of faith in the coming inheritance:

> *'Ask of me, and I will surely give the nations as Thine*
>     *inheritance,*
> *And the very ends of the earth as Thy possession.'*
>                                                         (Psalm 2:8)

There are many occasions, especially in the burnt lands of Europe, where this political, deceptive spirit has been given ground to establish itself in Church and society, aiming to teach and persuade Christ's love slaves into immorality of all kinds and idolatry. There must be those who rise up against her deceptions and manipulation! Indeed, we should clearly see that the words of the Lord convict those who only tolerate Jezebel. Not follow her, or promote her. The Lord is speaking to those of us who know she's active, but prefer to keep our heads down. We must remember that compromise leaves us open to another stronghold also! But as we get into this heavy-duty warfare, we really must train ourselves both to submit to the piercing gaze of the Son of God who has eyes *'like a flame of fire'* and feet *'like burnished bronze'* (Revelation 1:14, 15) and to receive that same sight from Him. He has walked through the fire of temptation, luring us to drift away from our first love, to fear, to other comforting doctrines that deaden us to sharp discernment. He has come through conquering, and to conquer. He is the overcomer! He has to search us and lead us for the sake of delivering whole nations and peoples, our inheritance, into the freedom of His marvellous love.

## Sardis or Philadelphia?

> *'And to the angel of the church in Sardis write: He who has the seven Spirits of God and the seven stars says this: "Wake up ... for I have not found your deeds completed in the sight of My God. Remember therefore what you have received... And to the angel of the church in Philadelphia write, He ... who has the key of David ... says this: "Because you have kept the word of My perseverance, I also will keep you ... hold fast what you have..."'*
>
> (Revelation 3:1, 2, 3, 7, 10, 11)

As the levels of pressure and opposition built up in these cities at the gates of Europe, we are presented with two city churches which are in direct counterpoint to each other. The context in which He talks to them both is one of completion, because there is an end of all things. The letter to Sardis refers to the seven Spirits of God and the book of life, images of completion and eternity. There is a similar sense in the letter to Philadelphia. He is coming soon. And the promises to those who overcome here are those of being established in the New Jerusalem, in the heavenly city at the summation of all things. The context is the same; the content could not be more different.

Sardis has a name for being a breakthrough city. The church there actually took over the temple to Artemis. Archaeological remains show a large temple building in which many Christian signs had been carved. It was a very prosperous city, near fertile plains and the church grew in like manner. From a human point of view, it was a good, strong and thriving church. But God, who is Spirit, with the angels, could see a different picture. He sees them as nearly dead and with an unfulfilled mandate. Unlike the other churches up to this point, any encouragement He has for them is left to the end, for the few people in Sardis who are continuing faithfully. His immediate word is an urgent, strident warning. There is no time left. It's now or never for them to wake up, and get back on the job.

Philadelphia by contrast has the feeling of being a struggling band with 'only a little power', and for them any time left is probably too long! *'I am coming quickly; hold fast!'* is their encouragement. But they are honoured. There is not even a hint that anything need be any different at all. These are overcoming truly, because they are persevering.

In the face of the strongholds being established in these cities, the Church is called to rise up and war. We have to war in the heavens by authoritative prayer and on the earth by disciplined holiness. We have to be wise and discerning in the subtle temptations that will take us captive. We have to love God passionately, commit to Him whether by life or death, and by the Spirit, so feed on the Word and revelation of God that we are securely armed for the fight. But this is for the long haul. We know there will be a climax to history, but we don't know when. And this is the pen-ultimate great weapon of the Enemy. Will we keep on keeping on?

We wrote earlier of the significance, particularly at this transitional moment in Europe, of perseverance. It is a hall-mark of an apostolic people. It is a mark of the nearing of the end of the age. *'When the Son of Man comes, will He find faith on the earth?'* (Luke 18:8). It is a requirement for overcomers. But how should we persevere?

We must continue in the same way that we began. *'Remember therefore what you have received and heard; and keep it'* (Revelation 3:3). The church in Philadelphia seemed to continue both in an understanding and experience of grace and the context of a final goal and end.

> *'I have put before you an open door ... I will make them to come and bow down at your feet ... I have loved you ... I also will keep you ... I am coming quickly ... '*
>
> (Revelation 3: 8, 9, 10, 11)

It is the Lord who is taking all the initiatives towards the completion of all things. Even when He commends them for keeping the word, it is of *'My perseverance'*. Pressure often leads to striving, but Philadelphia had learned the secret of persevering in the fullness of God's provision for God's battle. It is He who has the key of the Kingdom. Called the key of David, it connotes for us his wild abandon to the purposes of God. He was the man who was after God's own heart. He never denied God's calling and faithfulness to him. Like the church at Philadelphia, he never denied His name.

The problem in Sardis was that they were, seemingly, successful. Now God had already warned His ancient people what might happen when they came into the land – that they might settle successfully. They also were to

> *'Beware lest you forget the Lord your God . . . lest, when you have eaten and are satisfied . . . and when your herds and your flocks multiply . . . then your heart becomes proud and you forget the Lord your God . . . you may say, "My power and the strength of my hand made me this wealth." But you shall remember the Lord your God, for it is He who is giving you power . . . '*
>
> (Deuteronomy 8:10, 12, 14, 18)

They also were to remember how they received it. They, and we, received life and power, authority and destiny, by free grace from God. And for the purpose of pressing through in all the earth with the revelation of His blessing to all people! But in their wealth and growth, they were in danger of forgetting the source and means whereby they were blessed. And they were forgetting the purpose. They were denying His name. If this is not a word that strikes to the heart of the European experience, we don't know one that is! Christian nations, blessed and established by the grace of the gospel, we became proud, greedy and lazy. We stopped sowing in gratitude to the spiritual source of our development. We foolish Europeans! Who has bewitched us? Were we so foolish? Having begun in the Spirit, were we now being perfected in the flesh? (Cf. Galatians 3:1–3.) The stronghold of Sardis became the stronghold in Europe.

And the hope of any redemption is first to repent, and then to learn to live again by the Spirit and in the spiritual places, in the light of the final great Day. Jesus holds the stars and has the seven Spirits of God. When He commends those who do stay faithful, He promises to confess them before His Father and the angels. We are enjoined to live from His spiritual standpoint and behave in the seen realm as if totally connected to His eternal reality and destiny. His reference to confessing us before the angels resonates with His teaching in Matthew's Gospel:

> *'Therefore do not fear them, for there is nothing covered that will not be revealed ... And do not fear those who kill the body ... but rather fear Him who is able to destroy both body and soul in hell ... Everyone therefore who shall confess Me before men, I will also confess him before My Father who is in heaven ... And he who does not take his cross and follow after Me is not worthy of Me.'*
>
> (Matthew 10:26, 28, 32, 38)

It is inevitably a confrontational lifestyle at the interface of kingdoms! It is not enough to receive mercy and grace and then be content to enjoy the good things of the world while it careers towards hell and destruction. We have a mandate, to see God's Kingdom come on earth and His will done as in heaven. These are the deeds we must complete. Jesus really is aiming to sum up all things, to complete the process of the revelation of His grace and mercy being expressed throughout the earth, *'and then the end shall come'* (Matthew 24:14). Once again in Europe, in His kindness and mercy, He is setting before us an open door. We are to repent, and then live and act, equipped by grace, in the great cosmic battle of all time. Urgently. Right through to the end.

## Laodicea

*'The Amen, the faithful and true witness, the Beginning of the creation of God, says this ... "Behold I stand at the door and knock; if anyone hears My voice and opens the door, I will come in to him, and will dine with him and he with Me. He who has an ear, let him hear what the Spirit says to the churches." '* (Revelation 3:14, 20, 22)

The one who is the Amen, who will sum all things up, reconciling them to Himself by the blood of His cross, will do so because He is faithful and true. Even when we are faithless, the Scripture assures us that He remains faithful because He cannot deny Himself. The picture of the Laodicean church is the one that we Europeans know so well. It is the hopeless one. Neither hot nor cold. With some present but mainly historical reference to the gospel, we are not entirely cold. We have nevertheless managed to contain and dilute the marvellous power of the freely laid down life of God Himself, till we are quietly complacent. Not hot with passion and zeal. Though we don't really feel rich, in global terms economically and culturally we are abundant and, certainly as British, prefer not to have need of anyone! Still His faithfulness has a way of restoration. Even in the face of the most complete sell-out to Mammon over the years, the stronghold of the western world, God is determined to win us back.

So His advice to us is to buy what we need. We need gold refined by fire. We have already seen that the feet of Jesus are like burnished metal refined as through a fire. Jesus is our purified glory. He has taken our individual and corporate humanity and history to the cross to be purified in the suffering of death. We need white garments, the good deeds prepared beforehand that we should walk in them. It is Jesus who incarnated goodness. His are the purest deeds – the healing touch for the outcast leper, the food for the hungry, the cleansing of the temple. He has prepared the means for us to follow, in the Holy Spirit given to us. We need eye salve so we can see. It was Jesus who spat into the dust and created the paste that healed blindness. He mixed His own moisture with the dirt from which we were made to give new sight. We need Jesus.

But Jesus is the free gift of God. Salvation is not by works, or anything that we have, but by grace alone through faith. What does this instruction to buy mean? This was the conflict for the one known as the rich young ruler (see Luke 18:18–24). Everything about Jesus was what he wanted. He loved His words, His life, His kindness and His power. He wanted to be like Him and to be with Him. But he was rich and blind to his own self-righteousness. Jesus stood before him, in open invitation to begin again, to taste His marvellous faithfulness, to come with Him into the Kingdom of God and His righteousness, to be saved from all the lost opportunities, regrets and fears. But he was rich and blind to his own self-righteousness.

Jesus looked at him and loved him.

> *'Those whom I love, I reprove and discipline; be zealous therefore and repent.'*                          (Revelation 3:19)

The young man went away very sorrowful for he was unable to pay the price necessary for the free grace of Jesus to be effective for him. It seemed an impossible thing to ask.

This brings us full circle. It is impossible for European nations to taste again the kindness of the Lord since

> *'... in the case of those who have once been enlightened and have tasted of the heavenly gift ... and have tasted the good word of God and the powers of the age to come, and then have fallen away, it is **impossible** to renew them again to repentance.'*                          (Hebrews 6:4–6, our emphasis)

Since we have fallen away, we have given place to the massive strongholds evidently growing in the gates of the continent. We have lost our passion and love, become afraid, tolerated false teaching, given place to Jezebel. We have been found wanting again and again. We have failed to persevere in honouring the Lord's kindness and name. And we have become rich. All our political decisions are now based upon how much they will cost. Politically, the future shape of Europe will be decided on economic grounds alone, and Christians may well be among the most vocal in these arguments. How hard it is for the rich to enter the Kingdom of heaven!

But Jesus is the Amen. He will have the final word. He is the Beginning of the creation of God. We believe the Father wants to create a new thing in the lands of Europe at this moment in history, for the blessing of all the nations of the earth. He wants to bring into being a repentant, thankful people, ready to incarnate new reconciled relationships in the Holy Spirit. They will be of a new heart, with no aspirations to be known as anything but a friend of Jesus. They will love the land and share its groaning. They will love the Lord and be zealous for His righteousness. They will invade and stand in and through all spheres of creation, in the cities and the streets, the schools and the businesses, confident in prayer and bold against the Enemy. And they will love the poor. So they will live sacrificially and give radically. They will be church and church will be where they are. The apostles' teaching will be on all their lips. Prayer will be frequent and fervent, in cafés, canteens and classrooms. Fellowship will be deep between different nations, genders and generations. And the good news will catch like wildfire and the harvest will begin again in our nations.

Will we afford it?

If you have enjoyed this book and would like to help us to send a copy of it and many other titles to needy pastors in the **Third World**, please write for further information or send your gift to:

**Sovereign World Trust**
**PO Box 777, Tonbridge**
**Kent TN11 0ZS**
**United Kingdom**

or to the '**Sovereign World**' distributor in your country.

Visit our website at **www.sovereign-world.org** for a full range of Sovereign World books.